It Didn't Just Happen

by
Margaret DeLancey, R.N.

To the MacDonalds
from
Margaret DeLancey
August 22, 2010
Galatians 6:14

It Didn't Just Happen

Contact: Margaret DeLancey, R.N.
3250 State Road #476
Sellersville, PA 18960

Library of Congress Number: 2010907398
International Standard Book Number: 978-1-60126-235-6

Printed 2010
Masthof Press
219 Mill Road
Morgantown, PA 19543-9516

Table of Contents

It Didn't Just Happen

Things just don't happen to children of God,
They're part of a wonderful plan;
The troubles, reverses, the sorrows, the rod,
Are strokes of the Great Sculptor's hand.

When some dread accident strikes you a blow,
And you worry and fret and demand;
Why try so hard the mystery to know?
It's not just an accident; it's planned.

Have you been dropped from a place of power?
Do you wonder and reprimand?
Don't rebel, but look to Him in that hour;
This didn't just happen; it's planned.

Persecution, tribulation come down like a storm;
Friends disappoint and withstand;
At last, all alone, bewildered, forlorn,
You look, and He smiles: "This is planned".

Do you wonder why God to affliction should call,
And why you must suffer and moan?
"No man should be moved by afflictions" says Paul,
"For you know it is part of the plan."

Did some dear one sicken and finally die?
Did your heart break with anguish and woe?
Did you question your Lord, and cry: "My God-why?"
Don't question - He planned it just so.

Things just don't happen to children of God,
The blue print was made by His hand;
He designed all details to conform to His Son,
So all things that happen are planned.

No matter what happens to those called "His own",
Events that are awful or grand;
Every trial of your life He sends from His Throne;
Things just don't happen; they're planned.

ROMANS 8:28 - "And we know that all things work together for good to them that love God, to them who are the called according to His purpose."

May 5, 1950

Pastor H. E. M. Snyder
Newburgh, N. Y.

Since I became a Christian at the age of twenty-one, I have learned some wonderful doctrinal truths about the scriptures. (Note: all Biblical references are taken from the King James Version of the Bible.).

God knew us before the foundations of the world (Ephesians 1: 4) and He also knows us by name. (John 10: 3)

He knows my beginning and my end and has preserved my goings-out and my comings-in for over eight decades. During the eighty-two years of my life the Lord has brought me through many unusual circumstances. He has blessed me abundantly. What has happened in my life did not happen by chance or good luck.

My closest friends have often challenged me to write a book. I have pondered this for several years and now I want to share some of my experiences with you. Many thanks to family and friends who have encouraged and prayed for me. First of all I thank my daughter Rebekah who read each chapter and made significant suggestions. Dave helped me much with the computer projects and editing. John also helped and Dan was a prayer warrior. They all contributed their stories in one of the chapters.

In the writing field I am thankful for the encouragement of Mrs. Edna Kruse who chairs our small writers club in our retirement community. She also told me about the Writers Conference at Montrose Bible Conference grounds in Pennsylvania. I was exposed there to my new wonderful world of writers and publishers.

Finally, I praise the Lord for giving me thoughts in the night, inspirations during the day, and strength to complete the task.

I dedicate this book to my four wonderful children:

David Jonathan DeLancey, BA,
Captain United States Navy
Rebekah Eleanor DeLancey, BA, ME'd, C.P.
Daniel Ellis DeLancey, BA
John Thomas DeLancey, BA, M.Div, D.min

Soli Deo Gloria

The Wash Basin

Actually I have never seen the original wash basin but it played a vital role in the birth of many babies. If it could talk it would have stories. As my mother related to me, the proud owner of this antique was Margaret Weissert-Wunderley. She prized the vessel because she used it for very special events. When she heard that a mother was in labor she wrapped the pottery basin in a large towel and started out on foot. Carrying the heavy basin was a struggle as she trudged through the poorly paved and narrow streets of the small borough where she lived. Recently I discovered that many times she acted as a midwife. Those were the years when mothers didn't go to the hospital but had their babies in their homes.

One Sunday evening, on March 25, 1928, a little baby girl came crying into the big and wonderful world. The drama took place in a front bedroom with the family doctor attending. Margaret bathed the baby with great pride. This was her first grandchild.

The little baby was named Margaret Belle Wunderley. This is her story as I remember it.

The House Bill Built
CHAPTER 1

My father was William George Wunderley, always known as "Bill". He was determined to build a house for his bride, Alma Rosella Elliot. They moved in AFTER they were married. The floor wax was still a little bit tacky and with no cooking pots yet, they cooked eggs in the percolator! It really didn't matter. They were in their own love nest. Brothers and sisters came along after me—William Edward, Reuel Pardee, Roselaine Gertrude, Robert David and Faith Flora. With mother—no nicknames! We had a great time!

So vivid in my mind:

My father came home from the grocery store once a week. He honked the horn, the back kitchen door flew open and we all ran to the car to help carry in a bag or two. That's when bread was ten cents a loaf! It was a weekly routine.

We always prayed at meal time. Usually it was my father who led in prayer. Our parents were godly Christians. There were some times when they had us sit together in the living room and he read from the big family Bible. To close our devotional time we all got on our knees and each one prayed.

Christmas Eve surprises were always special. We went to our grandparents' home on Christmas Eve day and early evening we came home to a house that smelled like pine. With glee we entered the dining room where we screamed with delight at the sight of a lighted Christmas tree. Of a German tradition, we gave gifts on Christmas eve; each child had a small pile of gifts. Sometimes the piles consisted of a new coloring book, crayons, an orange and some candy. One year, I did receive a Shirley Temple doll. Maybe it was because we were coming out of the depression by then? Every year we rushed into the sun parlor to see if "Santa" left little cans of fruit in the play kitchen cupboard our father crafted for us.

There were some hard winters. We walked through two to three feet of snow to get to school. The long stockings got

wet and snow went down into our boots. Wet or not, we sat through school until lunch time. Back to our house we trudged for an hour's lunch. Classes resumed at 1:00 PM, we stayed until 4:00 PM and eagerly ran out when the bell rang.

Elementary school ended with an eighth grade graduation. Competition was close with my two best friends, but somehow I "squeaked" through for first place honors. I wanted a watch so fervently but knew we were too poor to ever get one. Imagine my surprise when we arrived home after graduation ceremonies when I walked into the house all decorated with garden flowers and full of people! I was given a watch, a very prized possession. As for the ceremonies can you believe that our class learned and sang a patriotic cantata entitled "Spirit of Seventy-Six"? Our music teacher had much courage!

I was about twelve years old when I was hoping to go to our church camp—Camp Redstone. My parents were not sure they could afford the twelve dollars a week fee.

They decided to pray about it and just trust the Lord. So my registration was sent in and I packed to go. The whole family went along to see me settled in at camp. On the way home they had to go up a hill behind a truck. Suddenly they saw something fall from the back of the vehicle. The truck kept going. Daddy realized it was a bag of potatoes. The bag broke and potatoes rolled all over the roadway. No cars were coming, so he parked the car and everyone jumped out and started to pick up potatoes. It was a gift from God!. When the bag was filled—it came to fifty pounds! That would really help to feed the family. My parents often told how God provided for the family on that special day!

High school days were awesome. We went from a small borough to the city of McKeesport. Our freshman year we attended a Jr. High School requiring a four-mile hike each way. We left at 7:30 AM to get there by 9. Senior High was only two miles. A'Capella Choir, marching and concert band (clarinet), and editing our yearbook kept me busy.

In all of our growing-up years we had chores. No matter the age, we had assignments if it was only helping "do the deeshes". One special job I had when I was fourteen was to do the family wash every week. Our dear mother was in bed that year because of pneumonia and being pregnant with number six. She was in bed for over three months before my baby sister was born. It was wintertime, so all the clothes had to be hung up inside. I can still see the clothes hanging there in rows up and down the whole cellar area. As I look back it was great training for me to do such a responsible job. My Grandmother Elliott came and ironed the day after I washed. One day when she was there and we were all in school, my mother started to hemorrhage. Grandmother called the doctor and an ambulance

At Geneva Our Family 1944

was sent. By the time they arrived at the hospital, my mother had no pulse, but the doctor went ahead and did a Cesarean section in order to save the baby. The baby was lifted out and was fine. My mother started to have a weak pulse and showed signs of life. So she was treated and we prayed. On the third day when my father was talking to her through the oxygen tent he told her that she had to get better and have faith that God would heal her. He suggested that the baby be named Faith. God did raise her up and after three weeks, we had our mother back home. We were so excited to see our brand new baby sister. As I recall, I continued doing the family wash until mother was up and strong and able to do it herself. But you can be sure that we all still had our various jobs.

Summer times were fabulous. As a trial run, Daddy put up the big tent in the back yard and we would be allowed to "try it out" for one night. Then it was packed up in a trailer, along with a portable kitchen, all our bedding, kerosene stove, and clothing. The tent slept eight! Off we went, pulling a trailer, traveling five hours to go 150 miles. The speed limit was 35 mph! Two glorious weeks every year at Geneva-on-the-Lake, Ohio. We ran bare-foot, lived in our bathing suits and absorbed lots of sunshine. This was great one year when we all had residual coughs from whooping cough. We giggled when we got home. No more grass floors! We walked on solid wood floors in the house that Bill built!

And they squeaked!

Black Tar Bubbles
CHAPTER 2

Have you ever walked on a patched paved road when the hot sun makes the tar bubble? My memory takes me back to the days when we children learned that if you stepped right on the bubble you could hear it pop—just like bubble gum! So it was always great fun to "break bubbles" on the way to church. Church was just down the street two blocks. The fun thing to us must have been aggravating to my parents especially if we had on our new Sunday shoes. Each Sunday we walked with the constant reminder, "Watch out for those tar patches in the street."

Those quick walks to church developed into much longer walks on certain Sunday afternoons. What a special time it was when my father took me hand-in-hand on our assigned Sundays to our mission Sunday School. Most families in the thirties had no automobiles and if they had no church in their area, had no way to get to one. A few Christian adults decided to start a Sunday School in a neighboring township. It may have taken us an hour to get there. The program revolved around singing, praying, reading scripture and teaching. The days we went, my father taught. Then back we would walk to our little town and as I remember it seemed to be more downhill going home. Along with watching for tar bubbles I remember distinctly one Sunday when my new patent leather shoes made searing blisters on the back of my heels. Those are precious memories.

Walking on those asphalt roads were a challenge but it was the beginning of how the LORD started working in my life. My father taught me by example, "Go ye into all the world and preach the Gospel to every creature." We went only a few miles into the country, but it was the start of my keen interest in missions and telling others about the LORD. When you go out walking, watch out for those tar bubbles! The LORD might be working on you!

I'm So Sick!
Chapter 3

"Oh Mother! I'm so sick!" She turned from the passenger side of the front seat to see me as white as a sheet and heaving. My dear Grandfather Elliott was carefully driving us to the big city of Pittsburgh. It seemed to be taking so long. We drove so slowly from one traffic light to another, smelled the fumes from the steel mills sitting beyond the railroad tracks on our right. I was pondering what a country girl would do in a new big place. "Oops," out it came. What breakfast I had was all over the floor and me and half-way out on the curb when we finally stopped. *What was I doing? Leaving my father, mother, three brothers and two sisters and moving into a live-in nurse's training home for three years?* The change seemed overwhelming.

We finally arrived and were told to go to the second floor of the nurse's home and find a bed in the old nursery. Our home for now would be in the old hospital on the north side of Pittsburgh. There were six of us in one room- with one bathroom. Orientation took several days and soon we were acclimated to getting up early, riding twenty minutes on the bus at seven in the morning. Our classes were in the new Presbyterian Hospital in the Oakland District of Pittsburgh.

We had breakfast in the hospital and then went to the 13th floor for our classes. Once in awhile we were able to go home for weekends. What fun it was to do this and my family drove me back on a Sunday evening to get me there by ten o'clock. My siblings often coached my little sister Faith to start asking for ice cream on the way home and my parents would give in to her passionate pleas.

One weekend I didn't go home was a Christmas weekend. Christmas morning we all had to be at the hospital an hour early, all bright and shining in our "probie" uniforms.

Some forty of us were assigned to walk all the halls of the hospital to bring good cheer to the patients. From one end of the hall to another, with real burning candles, we sang many carols. This was a very emotional time for us, as we all wanted to be home for Christmas. Then we realized the patients wanted to be home too. The singing must have blessed many but we were the ones who were touched as tears ran down our cheeks. We carefully watched our candles so there would be no fire. Florence Nightingale would have been so proud of us!

I entered the elevator one day to go to class. Protocol called for students to go on last and always to stand at the back of the elevator. Doctors and head nurses were allowed to stand up front near the door. I aimed for the back, my arms loaded with books. As I turned to the front a man already on the elevator tapped me on the shoulder. I shrugged and tried to ignore him. Since I didn't give him attention, he took my shoulders and made me look right into his face. With a deep, melodic voice he said, "I guess you're a student nurse?" Instruction for all of us was to never flirt and always be PROPER so I didn't respond. The elevator stopped at the seventh floor and he walked off. The door closed and my classmates yelled, "Wunderley, didn't you know that was Bing Crosby?"

I had no clue who he was. We lived in the country and rarely went to the movies. (We did see "Snow White" and "Pinocchio".) That was about the exposure I had to the film industry. Very soon the famous man was inundated with nurses and visitors wanting autographs. He was there to visit one of his Pirate's baseball players—a first baseman, Elby Fletcher. The crowd crushed on Bing and the police were called and they ushered him safely out of the hospital. That evening some of my classmates suggested and then helped me to mark my uniform with indelible ink—so I would remember the date and time. I still have the uniform!

Nurses training at "Presby" was wonderful. In the 1940s, the surgeons were just beginning to do tedious brain surgeries and we were privileged to watch from the amphitheater. Often we then had post-op care of the same patients; there were no intensive care units then.

As I look back, those years went fast and they were precious moments of my life. State boards took three days and we didn't have computers. We were tested on every subject we had studied. I think now, "How did I do it?" But most of us passed and I praise the LORD now for all those early morning rises and those all night duties. I didn't want to be a teacher like my mother because I thought I would need too much patience. Little did I know how trying some experiences would be and how much patience we needed every day. That skinny ninety-two pound brunette who vomited her first day on her way to Presbyterian Hospital School of Nursing got through her three years and is now telling you about it. From being sick herself to helping the sick was soon the agenda for each day. God was behind the scenes moving me to the most important "Day of Decision."

Did It Just Happen?

Chapter 4

Along with my nursing school studies I was serving in a leadership role with a major denomination. Involved in youth ministries, I had responsibilities in our local district of sixty-four churches, in our state programs, and also in the conferences on the national level. One Sunday evening I was giving a report in one of the large university churches. In the audience was a young Christian dental school student named Donald Ellis DeLancey. He said in his heart, "I want to meet that girl". We did meet in a college fellowship meeting after the evening service. We became great friends. After he graduated I still had some months to finish my nursing requirements.

We corresponded after he graduated and came back home to the Philadelphia area and in his letters he often asked me if I was a Christian. In my heart I felt insulted. *Of course I'm a Christian! Look at all my wonderful church work!"*

In February 1949 he came by bus from Philadelphia to Pittsburgh to visit me and my family. He brought me a diamond ring and asked me to marry him. I kept it for one day and then gave it back. Inside me resentment brewed . *The nerve of him asking me if I was a Christian!* I decided that he was one of those religious fanatics and that I shouldn't marry him. Dejected, he went home, took the ring back, got a complete refund, and bought a small green four door Studebaker!

Months passed by. My nurses' graduation took place in May and he wasn't invited. My Mother was chagrined with my attitude. Six months later I was working as a graduate nurse in the maternity division of our local hospital. The phone rang one morning in November. I was still home since I worked the 3-11 shift. Don's mother was calling to inform me that he was very sick and kept saying in his delirium, "Call Margaret, call Margaret." I told her I was sorry to hear this and thanked her for calling.

Mother asked, "What was that all about"? I related what I heard and sat and pondered. "What if he would die? He's a nice guy. I guess I would feel bad if I didn't go to see him." Mother agreed I should go; in fact she must have helped me pack. I don't know where we got the money, but we bought a ticket for me to fly from Pittsburgh to Philadelphia.

When I arrived he was still at home and critically ill. When a doctor came, he rushed him by ambulance to the hospital. I decided to quit my job and stay with him and help with his care. Sometimes it took two or three nurses to care for this man who had a viral pneumonia and mononucleosis; the antibiotics were just coming on the market. There was no ICU at that time. He spiked a 105 fever for many days. The LORD did raise him up and after two weeks he was sent home to recuperate. Of course he was very weak.

By then I felt I could go back home and he suggested before I left that I go with him to a service at the Church of the Open Door in Philadelphia. His uncle promised to drive so we went there for a Sunday evening service. The choir opened the service with a wonderful Gospel song "At Calvary" and the words of the first lines were, "Years I spent in vanity and pride, caring not my Lord was crucified. Knowing not it was for me He died at

Calvary." Dr. Jack Murray led the singing that evening and I was so moved. Dr Paul Whiting from Calvary Baptist Church in New York City was the guest speaker. He preached about heaven and how to get there! Never before in my church experiences had I heard a message like that! The LORD convicted me so much I felt he was preaching right to me.

When we arrived back home we sat with his parents and watched a television program called "Youth on the March." Dr. Percy Crawford was the speaker and when he finished his message he pointed his finger to the TV audience. He said, "It was for you the Savior died!" I knew he was talking to me!

Don took me into a back bed room where we knelt down by his parents' bed and helped me step-by-step to see that I needed to ask forgiveness and also ask the Lord Jesus to be my Savior. "For whosoever shall call upon the name of the Lord shall be saved." Romans 10:13 He helped me pray and I became a new creature in Christ. The following week I went back home and in two months we were married!

Still individuals, we were now not unequally yoked but one in Christ. We both felt led to follow the LORD in water baptism and we were baptized together at the First Baptist Church at Fourth and Arch Streets in Perkasie, Pennsylvania. Many times we looked back and realized how the Lord had put us together. It didn't just happen!

Big Sky Country
Chapter 5

A skilled dentist, my husband, Dr. Don DeLancey, owed his country two years of some kind of service. He heard of an opportunity for him to work for the Department of the Interior at the Fort Peck Indian Reservation in Poplar, Montana. His application was accepted and we left for Montana in late June of 1953.

Excitement mounted as we drove over the Mississippi River, and heard the call, "Go west young man, go west"! Our little four door green Studebaker took us through the badlands and onto the plains. Finally we arrived in a little Montana town with no paved streets. The only pavement was the US highway #2 which stretched all across the state of Montana. Indeed—it was Big Sky Country!

We settled into a government house and with only the belongings our small car could hold, we made it our home. Discoveries led us to tears! The dentist who served before us moved out and transferred to the state of Alaska for another assignment. He graciously left an ironing board, dishes, curtains, cooking utensils, furniture—just everything that we needed and didn't bring along. I remember as we dropped to our knees, my precious Don praying and thanking God for His provision.

Other folks working in the hospital gave us advice. "We are not sure about the old chickens and the beef you buy at the local co-op so it is better for you to drive twenty-two miles each way to get your groceries." We did that every Saturday morning!

The first year we attended a small chapel on the highway. Just a few families met but it did grow. That first Christmas we organized twelve adults and six children into a singing group and the Chapel presented their first Christmas Cantata. What a happy celebration. The little chapel was packed with curious visitors. Our second year we helped the oil people from Arkansas organize the First Baptist Church of Poplar, Montana, and Don taught an evening series about the Tabernacle in the wilderness.

One day, Dr. DeLancey gave a gospel of John to one of his Indian patients. She was elderly and close to ninety years of age. She asked what it was that he had given her. He told her that it was a Gospel of John. She asked him to read John 14. He had not known that she was blind and could not read. He then

asked her how she knew the scriptures and she said that she had been married to the first missionary to the Sioux Indians. She remembered how they would not bury their dead but put them on an animal skin propped on four poles—up into the air maybe six feet. They believed that the "spirits" would come and take the body eventually. Of course, it would decay and cause contamination so the US Government did end this practice and asked for in-ground burials. It was our privilege to go to Lizzie Arthurs little smoke-filled cabin to read scriptures and to sing for her on lonely Sunday afternoons. Our only guest our first Christmas was Lizzie Arthur. She enjoyed especially eating the corn on the cob we had frozen and managed very well with her few remaining teeth. The following Christmas, we had another guest—"Caske", Sioux for "the firstborn" David Jonathan DeLancey.

How the Indians loved David! We took him around on his "papoose board" or in his baby carriage. The Indian children with runny noses and dirty hands wanted always to touch this brand new baby and they did when they thought we weren't looking. The Indian ladies made him a special quilt and that is when they named him "Caske". He did grow up into a healthy little boy who at fifteen months could say the names of many family members when we came back to the state of Pennsylvania.

We also brought home some other treasures. The Indian patients would speak of the "Buffalo Jump" way out twenty miles into the prairie. So one day we drove out of town in search of this well known Indian site. The Indians reported that they killed more buffalo by running them over a cliff. With a sharp knife they would go to each animal, cut their jugular and let them bleed. Then they would cut off the heads, take the carcasses back to their villages for hide and meat and organs, and leave the heads. Over time the heads were carried down into the river, some were buried right into the river bank. That first day we saw some horns sticking out of the mud. The following Saturday we took a young geologist and his wife and we excavated the river bank and found twenty-five buffalo heads. Local residents were excited about the exploits of "those green horn Pennsylvanians". Our largest skull measured twenty-eight inches from tip of horn to tip of horn. That one later traveled with me when I lectured on fossils in our Creation series. These digs all happened "before David".

Joyfully, both of our parents came to visit us to see their first grandchild. Other family members were Aunts Roselaine and Faith, Uncles Reuel and Robert.

Mondays after school brought the promise of many muddy feet. The children came running to attend the Children's Bible Club. Half-white American and half-Native American, they filled our small living room. A faithful Bible lady in town taught the lesson and I helped with the singing. In the social activity after, the boys especially wanted to play "Cowboys and Indians"!

The big sky country will never be forgotten! Nor will the fifty–six below temperature one day, the walks to the local armory to see the spirited basketball games, our first riding lesson when my horse wanted to stop in the middle of the river and roll over, the Indian dwellings across the street with grass growing out of the mud roofs, horses in our yard when we didn't close the fence. In the winter, making an ice pond in our back yard for ice skating. In the summer, attending our first real live rodeos!

Big sky country—oh yes! Those two years were precious.

The Home on the Hill
Chapter 6

"Two lots on a dirt road—for sale". It sounded good. Don and I looked and bought them. The farmer who sold us the property volunteered to cut down all the overgrowth. With no fire restrictions then, we had at least a half dozen fires burning at one time. Covered with sweat and smoke, we delighted to be the new owners. One year later we purchased two more lots below the first ones.

In January 1956 the builder dug the foundation and by October we moved into our new home where I lived for over fifty years. Sporting temporary wood sidewalks, we welcomed visitors from the very start.

On February 28, 1957, God gave us a thrilling gift, a sweet baby girl. I remember holding her in a rocking chair when she was only a few days old. As I held Rebekah Eleanor the tears ran down my face. I sobbed to my mother, "Isn't she wonderful?" With an understanding heart she said that she felt the same way when each of her six children were born. She understood about my great joy.

David and Rebekah enjoyed our big yard. They saw us digging and planting, watering, and mowing. David like the flowers and one time pulled out a handful of daffodils, roots and all, to give to his mother. I am not sure about Rebekah's interest then, but in her middle age years, she is an avid gardener.

We wanted more children and two were never born. One died at six weeks, and one at four months. Along with seeing the LORD when I get to heaven, I also anticipate the joy of meeting two children I have never seen. Then it happened! The doctor said that I was pregnant again.

We went from one trimester to the next one and I stayed pregnant until three weeks before my scheduled due date. Then I was very sick, toxic and vomited often. I only gained six pounds. The doctor came to the house every day to give me an injection for the gastric upset. "You will be fine when the baby comes." No one took ultra sounds those days and only one heart beat was heard. I went into a prolonged labor and finally Daniel Ellis was born. Twenty four minutes later, my nurse friend called to the doctor. "We have another baby coming!" Out came John Thomas. Don had gone home to check on David and Rebekah. Fathers were not allowed in the delivery room in that era. The doctor called him at our home and asked if Don was sitting down? His news was, "You have twin boys!" Their delivery and the following days were so unusual that we wrote the following:

Twins!
Valley of the Shadow!
Life! Death!

What opposites! But truly they worked together in my life in February of 1961. On Tuesday evening, February 21st, my body was delivered of not one tiny baby, but of two beautiful baby boys! A double blessing and a thrilling surprise to all of us. Daniel, the first to enter the world, responded to the skilled care of an excellent pediatrician and after having difficulty breathing, showed signs of improvement. He is now as active and as hungry as his brother John, who came 24 minutes later.

But you ask, why associate the Valley of the Shadow of Death to this happy story? Dear reader, along with carrying twins, I was the victim of an insidious disease—Infectious Hepatitis. I remained in serious condition until Friday of that same week when, due to capillary hemorrhages of the upper intestinal tract, I fell to the critical list and into shock. My blood pressure dropped to 60/40 (normal is 120), pulse rose to 140 (normal is 72) and body temperature dropped to 94 (normal is 98). I felt my life ebbing away as a fine team of doctors and nurses worked rapidly with the best of modern emergency treatment.

Fear was not present for I knew as the Apostle Paul has written—"To be absent from the body and to be present with the Lord." (11 Corinthians 5: 8)—that I too would go to be with the Lord. You ask—how can this writer be so sure? I know that one day when I was 21 years of age I realized that I was a sinner, and that there was no good thing in me. The scriptures say, "For there is no difference: for all have sinned and come short of the glory of God." (Romans 3:22, 23) We also read in Jeremiah 17:9, "The heart is deceitful and desperately wicked."

There is no worldly remedy for sin. Sin is a disease of man's soul and many people try to cure this disease and ease their conscience by trying to do good works, do social work, join a church and pay dues every year, be kind to others, help the poor, and do other charitable things. These are all fine human efforts, but man cannot find a true way to God through any but the Lord Jesus Christ. It was the death of our wonderful Lord on the cross that gives us the real cure for sin. I had accepted the cure, had taken the Lord as my personal Savior, and had assurance in my heart that He would take me Home. Christ promises in John 6: 47, "Verily, verily, I say unto you, he that believeth in Me hath everlasting life."

At 12:45 PM that day a praying friend in the Lord walked into my room. She, also a nurse, asked, "How do you feel, Margaret?" I faintly replied, "I think I'm dying." She realized that my life was in the Lord's hands, but could not humanly speaking, see me leave my husband and now four children. Quickly she said, "Margaret, you'll have to fight. Someone might be saved through this." Quietly I told her to hold my hand and pray harder than she ever prayed before. "The effectual fervent prayer of a righteous man availeth much…" (James 5:16) I am sure she was sent of the Lord for she was the first one to pray and God heard her prayer. Then came my husband's mother and she also prayed. She smiled at me and said, "The Lord raised the dead—He can heal the sick." My husband was called from his professional office and my family was called from 300 miles away where prayer was also constantly sent to the Throne of Grace. With grief stricken hearts they waited to see the hand of the Lord through modern medicine, slowly pull me back to the realms of earth.

Since my critical days it has been made known to us that from the body of the Christian student nurses, from the groups of many area and distant churches, from the lips of a great number of listeners to a local radio station which spot announced a need for prayer, from the special meetings called in my behalf, came the prayers of God's saints that His will be done in my life. Three days later, a fourth pint of blood was slowly running into my veins. The doctors expected the hemoglobin count to be up to 10 grams that Sunday morning (it had dropped to 6.5 grams due to the hemorrhage). The laboratory report was phoned to the nurses' station by 11 AM just as the churches were having prayer for me, and the report was that the hemoglobin was up to 11.7. Thus there was no need for the fifth pint of blood which had been ordered. This was just one of the many laboratory reports as my convalescence progressed. Day by day the Lord has added strength and I am back to normal health again.

Dear reader, if you have never accepted this cure for sin—if you would die today, are you ready to meet your God? He has given you physical life, sustains it with the very air you breathe, but will some day also take your life from you. If you had been in my place, what would have happened to your soul? Christ stands at your heart's door TODAY and longs to enter in, be your cure for sin and your everlasting Savior. Why don't you see yourself as a sinner, bow your head and ask Him to enter TODAY? TODAY is the day of salvation; tomorrow may be too late.

And dear reader, if you are a Christian, isn't it wonderful to know that the Lord cares for us? He knoweth each sheep by name and knows our every need. Truly the Lord is good. David writes in Psalms 34: 19, "Many are the afflictions of the righteous, but the Lord delivereth him out of them all." The Lord has truly delivered me and through this wonderful experience my testimony is, "For he that is mighty hath done to me great things and Holy is his name." (Luke 1:49)

The above was written in a leaflet form and distributed to many for the first few years after the twins were born. It has been reprinted here as part of my story.

As I look back on that experience, it is encouraging to remember how God spared my life and gave me the privilege of being a Mother to four wonderful children.

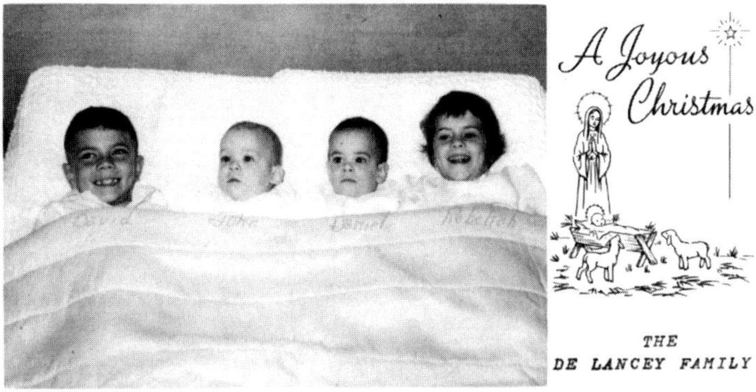
A Joyous Christmas
THE
DE LANCEY FAMILY

HOME

by Margaret DeLancey

Home is a place where you lay your head —
Home is a place where the children are fed.
Home is a refuge in these days of dread.
"There's no place like home" — the poet has said.

But our thoughts wonder as we think of one
Who had no Home — when He did come.
"No room!" — the inn keeper cried that night.
And so to the stable they went in their plight.
Mary did lay in a bed of hay —
And gave birth to a child that Christmas Day.

That child grew and when time came —
He laid down His life — but not in vain.
For you and me who were dead in sin —
He died — so a heavenly Home we'd win.

This Christ is back in His beautiful place
Somewhere beyond in the reaches of space.
Preparing mansions beyond compare
Of any such dwelling we see here.
These will but crumble and we'll leave them behind;
The believers will go to a Home so sublime.

So as Christmas time comes and our Home is full
Of laughter, of scurry, of work and of school —
We send you our greetings, our thoughts and our prayers
That Christ be in your hearts, your Home and your cares.

Have a Happy and a Blessed Christmas

One Room Schoolhouse
Chapter 7

Seven miles out of the town of Perkasie, on a back road, an empty one-room schoolhouse sat vacant. The gray stone was still in good condition, outside paint needed attention, and the doors were locked for years. The bus driver of our town church had a vision to open it and use it for a Sunday school. Some older people in the town church were dubious about such a project. How would we ever pay the rent? Don and I, members of the town church, had just received a prayer letter from a fine pioneer missionary couple in the country now called Bangladesh. They were spending their nights in soggy sleeping bags on river banks as they wended their way north to reach the Tripura Tribe. My husband's heart was challenged. He told the congregation, "We can certainly go north seven miles in our comfortable cars to open a Sunday School! I will pay the first three months rent and let us just see what the LORD will do."

Teams of volunteers went from door-to-door with invitations. Down one lane and up another we went. Some folks promised to come and some did come out of curiosity.

Preparation began. We unlocked the schoolhouse and started to work. Teams of willing workers took down the cob webs, cleaned the walls, washed the windows, and scrubbed the wood floors. The heat unit stood guard at the side of the

one and only entrance door. It proved adequate but I wonder about the safety codes back in the 1950's. There was a nursery in the back corner of the one big room, protected only by a two-sided curtain.

The first Sunday, the bus came and unloaded the passengers who usually went to the town church. Others who lived on the surrounding back roads timidly entered. Don had been elected by the town church to be the first Sunday School superintendent. When he opened the first Sunday meeting he challenged us to start memorizing the first chapter of the Gospel of John. We added a new verse each Sunday. The attendance for that first Sunday was over forty people. Eight adults came from the mother church to fill leadership roles. The name of the new ministry was Rockhill Baptist Chapel.

As the LORD blessed a student pastor was called. He served while he was in seminary. Then another seminary student came to take the leadership. The mother and the daughter churches met together to form a separate independent congregation now known as Bethel Baptist Church.

There was only a crawl space under the building. With good engineering and careful excavation, a basement was built. It was a fine meeting room and held our Primary department of the Sunday School. At our saturation point, we had eighty children sitting back to back in their separate classes.

With strong pastoral leadership a new educational building was built behind the school and the rest is history. The church has grown tremendously and they have a large Christian School during the week. The campus has been greatly expanded.

Don faithfully served as one of the two deacons. He also taught Sunday School and used his musical talents to serve the LORD. I directed the music education and the choirs. We served there for twelve years and then returned back to the mother church. The Lord, by this time, was leading us into a very special field—"Creation Evangelism". The doors for this ministry opened wide!

In the Beginning—Evolution?

CHAPTER 8

I don't think so! "I don't want my children learning this," declared my husband as he boldly marched into the office of our supervising principal. Don was protesting the strong evolutionary teaching in our public schools in the early seventies. Our oldest son Dave came home with a chart of the so-called fossil men. Each one was described, telling how many millions of years ago they lived. On the top of the page it read, "These are our ancestors." This certainly defied the concept that God had created us.

The principal said we could have our children excused from viewing any of the evolutionary films. One of the teachers who was there for our interview with the principal became very irate. In fact, the next morning the teacher called my husband at seven o'clock and said he planned to take my husband to the American Civil Liberties Union. To be awakened with news like this was a startling jolt. Don talked calmly to him and further explained our position. The conversation ended and we waited and prayed. As days and weeks went by no action was ever taken. Courteous greetings were exchanged if we met on the street or at athletic events. Perhaps it was only a threat?

Many years later in January of 1997, I arrived home from a missions trip to Papua New Guinea where I had taught some of the missionary kids. There were many calls on my answering machine and I began to listen to the messages. I trembled as I heard the voice of this same school teacher. *What did he want? My husband is in glory. He can't confront him now. Is he after me?* I prayed and with trepidation dialed his number. To my astonishment he wanted me to come to his church and teach two one-hour classes on Creation for a group of about fifty people. I was overwhelmed at how God works. He knows our hearts, our thoughts, our motives and the thoughts and intents of our hearts. He can change our minds and reveal to us His power. No longer hostile, the teacher was very receptive and appreciated the material we presented. It was a lesson to me how we need to stand on our convictions and not compromise. It is our job to witness. It is God who gives the understanding and the victory.

About the same time as our earlier confrontation, we became aware that there was an organization called the Associates for Biblical Research. This group of pastors and scientists could help us refute this false dogma of evolution. We attended some of the meetings and met the founder Dr. David Livingston and his sweet wife Esther. Dr. Livingston taught us much about taking a stand for Scientific Creationism.

Dr. Livingston also directed studies in Israel in the field of Biblical Archaeology. One of the most exciting times in our lives was spent as we participated in our first archaeological dig at King Herod's winter palace in the ancient city of Jericho, Israel. Don was invited to serve on the ABR board of directors. That entailed going to the regular board meetings and the wives would go along for the fellowship. I often look back on those precious days and remember how the LORD used ABR to encourage us in our ministries. Don served on the board until the LORD called him home. In fact, one of the last visitors to come and see him in the hospital was Dr. Livingston.

Another organization called "Bible Science" also influenced our ministry. Directed by Rev. Walter Lang, this group also had a teaching ministry. We packed up our family and along with our sleeping bags, flew to Caldwell, Idaho, to attend a Family Creation Conference. During the day we had classes and also field trips when we scouted through the mountains. One afternoon our families followed Rev. Lang for a hike and climb up to the highest peak in the whole area of the Sawtooth Mountains. The goal was to reach the wooden cross that a group had planted there many years before. Rev. Lang led the pack but soon the younger ones sprung ahead making their own trails. As we started to reach a higher elevation where there was no trail and loose gravel, another attendee, a pastor, and I had to stop. We were not equipped for mountain climbing, and decided to retreat back down the mountain. We waited at the base of the mountain until twilight. Then it got dark and we began to be concerned for our families getting lost on the mountain. We wondered if we would have to call in a rescue team. We waited and waited and soon we heard a few voices, then a few more and eventually the hikers came back. After an hour of darkness everyone had returned. Rev. Lang was such a great trouper as well as a fine lecturer. In years to come we entertained him in our home as he traveled and lectured.

In the same conference we sat under the tutorship of Dr. Duane Gish. Dr. Gish is listed in American Men of Science and Who's Who in the West. He is a member of the American Chemical Society, the American Association for the Advancement of Science, and is a fellow of the American Institute of Chemists. Dr. Gish received his Ph.D in biochemistry in 1953 from the University of California, Berkeley. In 1971 he left the Upjohn Company to join the faculty at the Christian Heritage College. The name was later changed to the Institute for Creation Research and he has been the Associate Director and Vice President since that time. He often was our mentor when we would call upon him for answers to complex questions. In February 1999 I was a guest of ICR and stayed with Dr. and Mrs. Gish. One of those days they took me to the famous San Diego Zoo where we viewed many kinds of God's wonderful creatures- all uniquely designed! Dr. Gish is known as the foremost creation debater in the world today.

In the earlier years of learning, we realized that to reject a theory we had to be knowledgeable about what we were refuting. So we began to learn and then to share about the marvels of Special Creation. My husband answered invitations to lecture on the subject. Even today I meet folks who remember that he came to their church to speak. A month before his heart surgery, he was one of the speakers at the National Sunday School Convention in Washington, DC. His lecture room was full, and people stood outside in the hall, so they could get inside for the next session. Little did I know that when he went to glory on March 2, 1986, that the LORD would pass on to me the privilege of teaching in schools, camps, and churches. In the following seventeen years the LORD blessed me as I served him in this Creation Ministry.

The Day our Hearts Cried

Chapter 9

In the thirty-six years of marriage we shared many delightful times of travel and learning. One memorable time was when we traveled to Israel the second time. At the end of our tour there, we left the group and traveled alone on an extension trip to Egypt. We photographed many ruins and investigated tombs in the Valley of the Kings. In the Valley of the Queens we viewed Queen Hatshepsut's palace. One day Don counted and said we climbed up and down 1000 steps. It was all very fascinating but we never did forget the one day we spent in Luxor, Egypt, when our hearts cried.

A lazy polluted Nile River ribboned its way past the green bank of the city of Luxor. In the high eighties, it was a balmy day. We found ourselves four hundred miles south of Cairo in Upper Egypt. The plane departure time was later that evening, so we had time to saunter along the street. Horse-drawn carriages loaded with tourists passed by. We needed the exercise, so we chose to walk. With amusement we noticed a street sweeper machine coming along behind, cleaning up the organic deposits of the horses. Ambling along a narrow sidewalk we glanced at an opening of a tiny room. Inside a lady sat on a small bed. Underneath the bed several chickens were scratching for a morsel of food. Then we came to an open fire right there on the walkway. A pot hung over the fire and some kind of tar like substance was brewing. We thought maybe it was some kind of glue material the carpenter used in his shop next door.

As we made our way along the very narrow sidewalk, a young mentally challenged man with distorted facial movements staggered by. At first we were repulsed and then with second thought we were full of emotion for this dear young man. Do we remember that Christ healed a lunatic and had compassion on him? If only he could get some help and love and affection. He seemed to just be out roaming in the streets.

Then we looked down as we felt a little boy about four or five years of age tugging at our clothing. This little tot kept pulling at our jackets as he marched right along beside us not missing a step. His big brown eyes entreated as he repeated over and over and over again, "Pencils, Pencils, Pencils!" We had no pencils! So many pencils rested back home in our desk and junk drawers. If we only had known. How happy we could have made him! At least a dozen flies rested on his forehead, cheeks and chin. He made no attempt to shoo them away. After almost the length of a city block he stopped following us and guilt overwhelmed us.

A few more steps and we stopped short. There was a dead animal right there on the sidewalk. We almost stepped on it! The body looked like a cat and it was decaying with swarms of flies feasting. No effort had been made to take it away. To our right on the street a black veiled lady with a large load balanced on her head swiftly passed by. Another lady came along with a child sitting on her shoulder; the child rested his elbow on her head. Donkey carts darted here and there.

A gate coming up on the left aroused our interest. The sign read "Valley of the Kings Elementary School—Welcome." We ventured in and were met by two teachers. They went to get the headmaster who graciously took us from room to room. Grade one was crowded with three children in one seat. When we entered everyone stood at attention. What precious children!

The next room was the music class. Somehow we conveyed to them with the teacher's limited English and no knowledge on our part of Arabic that they should sing for us. Fifty little Arab children smiled and sang. Their eyes twinkled as they performed for us white haired Americans. Then it was our turn and I sang for them. What should I sing? The only thing that came to mind was "Jesus Loves Me". When I came to the chorus, "Yes, Jesus loves me", I choked up and could hardly finish without crying. They looked up at me with such beautiful eyes and wonderment. If they only had a missionary to tell them about Jesus!

The principal then took us to the cooking room, the shop room and then the sewing room. One little fifth grade girl went to the wall and took down a piece of embroidery that she had on display and insisted that I take it. Indeed, we brought it home and framed it and it is one of our cherished possessions. What a blessing that we saw the "Welcome" sign and dared to venture into the school grounds.

Back in the market place we observed the people. Busy merchants at their street shops. Women, hiding behind their black veils. Such beautiful eyes and pretty smiles—these were not disguised. These women marry and have children, work hard and serve their families. On a previous day, we saw women washing their clothes in an irrigation ditch while dead chickens floated by in the same water. And we complain that we "have to wash" and we have automatic washers!

Another day we went on a ferry across the Nile to see more of the ancient ruins. As we waited for the boat, we saw a man wading in mud up to his knees, using the mud along with donkey manure and straw. What was he doing? Making bricks! With rain there only two days a year can we imagine the hardships? But by the grace of God there go I! We saw children, daddies, mothers, we assume many without Christ. And we sit in our comfortable homes with many modern conveniences, yes, even dishwashers, and don't count our blessings. In such comfort we forget that the LORD commanded us to "Go ye into all the world and preach the Gospel."

Yes, our hearts cried that day for a people in a dark land. How can they hear without a preacher?

You Did What?
CHAPTER 10

When we came back from Israel and Egypt in the spring of 1983, we settled back into the routine of the dental office. Don had gone to the office and started with his first patient. I always stayed behind to do the extra duties at the house. I called my neighbor, a fine Mennonite local pastor to see if he had any problems as he watched our home. He assured me there was no problem and each day he had checked; everything was fine. I continued to do my daily chores, put the dog out, brought him back in, gave him water, made the lunches, unplugged the toaster (a safety must), brushed my teeth, went to the garage, got into the car and backed up. The only thing about this last procedure is that I forgot to open the garage door! I heard the shattering of glass everywhere from the windows at the top. There was glass all over the floor. I ran inside to the phone and crying said - "Jim, I need you! I just went through the garage door." This pastor had just talked to me and he was shocked! He promised to come immediately.

Then I called my husband at the office. He said, "You did what?" and between sobs, I kept repeating what I had done. He asked, "Shall I come home?" I assured him that he should not; I would be OK. He had a patient in the dental chair, a Reformed Episcopal pastor. Very fine man that he was, he asked if he could go to the house to help me. Don assured him that this would be wonderful. So he came to the house and I had a Mennonite pastor on one side and a Reformed Episcopal pastor on the other side. They had their arms around me and I cried and cried and cried! They assured me that the door could be fixed and no one was hurt—not even the car. They swept up the glass. Then they asked me to back the car out. After a minute of thinking it over, they decided I should put the car back into the garage. I was in no condition to be out driving the car. The RE pastor said that he would take me to the office.

I will never forget that day! I cried between every patient and would not let them see my face, if I could help it. Between each patient, Don came into the x-ray room and put his arms around me. He didn't scold. He just loved me in my failure. I saw God's marvelous grace that day and I saw forgiveness on a human level. To be sure, my pride was broken. As the day went on, neighbors started to call me and tell me that someone must have tried to get into our house. "You should see your garage door! They must have rammed right through it to get inside." It was one of the saddest days of my life, but the garage door was fixed within a few days, and life went back to normal. The only thing that was changed was me. I saw the forgiveness and the love of God in my husband. The garage door repair man told me that men can do this also. He fixed a door of a large garage when the owner, a funeral director, pushed the wrong button and backed his hearse through a closed door. That story eased my broken spirit just a little.

God teaches us lessons in an unusual way. The story has entertained many friends as they heard what happened on that "jet-lag" day. I believe God has a sense of humor, too.

Psalm 2: 4 "He that sitteth in the heavens shall laugh."

Music
Chapter 11

"Music—a noun—organized tones in sequence and combinations which make up a continuous composition." That is what I found in my new Websters Notebook Dictionary. However formal the description is of this word, actual music came into my life at a very early age. With fond memories I can still see and hear my mother as she came into my room in the mornings. She went to the window, opened the blind as she sang to me:

Let a little Sunshine in
Let a little sunshine in
Clear the darkened windows,
Open wide the door,
Let a little sunshine in.

Another song that she sang to me was:

I had a little pony, his name was Dapple Gray
I loaned him to a lady to drive a mile away
She whipped him, she lashed him,
she drove him through the mire
I'll never let my pony go—for all the ladies' hire.

She started me early in life to have a song in my heart. My father liked to play the fiddle. When we had a childhood disease we were in bed for weeks at a time. We had no television or entertainment. But I recall my father coming into my small bedroom and playing "The Bear Went Over the Mountain" and singing the words.

By the time I was in second grade I wanted to take piano lessons. Alas—there was no piano. My kind neighbor, Mrs. Nickolls, living right next door heard of my plight. She said she would give us her piano! I will never know if she just gave it to us or if we did pay a sum of money. I was so excited! It was a player piano as well. I spent hours pumping those pedals and watching all those keys go up and down. There were times when Mother would say, "Now Margaret Belle, that's enough for now!"

My brother William and I started piano lessons. He and I walked down our street and turned left up Liberty Way to our teacher's house. Mrs. Martin herself was quite a pianist and when she played her hands were all over the keyboard as she bounced around on the piano stool. At twenty-five cents a lesson she gave us our "piano start".

I don't believe William followed suit, but along with the piano lessons, I sang in our church choir. Music reached into my soul. One Sunday, when we practiced before our church service, we sang a song about mothers. One verse was about mothers in heaven. I vividly remember crying and leaving the choir practice and running out of the church, up the street to my home to see if maybe my mother had died. She lovingly hugged me and assured me that she was fine.

In grade school we had a music teacher who came once a week. How we loved her! She had us singing little musicals, costumes and all!

During high school days I sang in choruses and my senior year was in the A'Capella choir. We sang two of our songs in Latin.

Nurse's training did not lend itself to taking time to sing, but one day a classmate and I saw a poster advertising an audition for the Bach Choir of Pittsburgh. As a lark, we decided to go and try out. We had to sing some scales, match tones, sight read a piece and to our surprise, were accepted. We sang one season with them performing "St. John's Passion" in the Carnegie Music Hall of Pittsburgh. In the rehearsals I marveled and listened to the professional soloists. They had so much talent and were so dynamic. It was such an honor to be there in that final concert.

As a new Christian I was asked to sing with two sisters, Marian and Sally Gahman in a gospel trio. We enjoyed that ministry in church and once in a while we sang on a local Sunday radio broadcast.

When we went to Montana to serve on the Indian reservation (see Big Sky country), I was asked to be pianist in this small church. Christmas was coming that first year we were there and in preparation I wrote to First Baptist Church in Perkasie and asked if they could loan their copies of a cantata we had done. They shipped the copies and we began our practice. It seemed impossible to me, but we went ahead with our plans. Twelve adults and six children worked hard. We had no other pianist so I had to play and direct. They were so excited as they sang "Star over Bethlehem". This little white chapel sitting on the only paved road in town, Highway 2, was full of happy people who never heard a cantata sung by these people who never sang in a choir! The choir had no great singers, maybe a monotone or two, but they rejoiced as they lifted up their voices. The church was full of visitors and the congregational singing was a thrill. It was a monumental evening.

Because there was no one else in this little town to teach piano, I had a few students whom I taught from the Beginner and Grade 1 piano lesson books. One gal seemed hopeless. I think she was more at home on her horse than on the piano bench.

When we came back to Perkasie Mrs. Lillian Ewing asked me to start a children's choir. She gave me vocal lessons over a long period of time (in between babies), and she was our choir director.

Then we were called to serve and help in our mission outreach—Rockhill Baptist Chapel. In the early days it was a "school house church" and there we had a small volunteer choir. There were four melody men who graced the back row of a group of twelve willing singers. Some didn't read music or parts, but they sang as unto the Lord.

That choir grew to over 40 people as we moved out of the school house and into the next building. We were now Bethel Baptist Church. There were not enough seats for all of us, so choir A sang one month and choir B sang the second month. We all rehearsed together and always had a full choir. If someone was absent in choir A, then someone came in from choir B. No empty seats. We added a Jr. choir, and a Children's Music Hour. The little ones were a joy as they sang:

We're busy, busy beavers
Busy every day
Winning souls for Jesus
As we go on our way.

My husband was a fine cornet player. He also played a trombone and an E flat horn. So, I never wanted for "Special Music".

After twelve years, we were led back to First Baptist Church in Perkasie. By this time, all of our children studied musical instruments. All took piano lessons, and Dave played trombone, Rebekah trumpet, Dan trumpet, and John, trombone. From time to time we played special musical numbers in church.

First Baptist asked me to be the choir director when there was a vacancy. It was then we started the ministry of Director of Music. The program included groups of many ages.

Children's Music Hour- Kindergarten to third grade

Jr. Choir- 4th through 6th grade

Jr. High Singers grades 7-9

Senior Choir 10th grade and older.

We did small programs with the children, not like what is happening today under the wonderful leadership of my successor, Darla Gruver-Mulhall. What they do now is just so phenomenal! The children learn and sing a full musical in just a matter of a few months.

Our church program kept us busy with a Sacred Concert once a year and special programs in the Christmas and Easter seasons. A favorite event was the "every five year" choir reunion when singers from yester-year returned. It involved an afternoon rehearsal, a meal, and then a concert of many voices! We were always blessed with so many voices singing praises to the LORD. What will heaven be like?

For almost two years we worked on memorizing hymns. We would pick a hymn a month and not use our books the last Sunday of the month. These were great hymns of the faith that still dwell in our hearts.

In 1983 I had a prompting from the Holy Spirit to resign as director. As I looked back on this decision, I felt it was of the Lord. I was then free to be a full time and caring wife and not be so caught up in ministry. It was in August of 1983 that my husband, Don, was playing in the Pennsylvania Senior Games Finals, in tennis (doubles), that he became sick and a few

1988 Choir Reunion—First Baptist Church, Perkasie, PA.

minutes later, had his first heart attack. I was then free to be his caring nurse and to help him through his recovery.

"God leads His dear children along."

Humor in the Church

We were all excited! The Junior High Singers were to present our "fantastic" twenty-minute Christmas Cantata.

Everyone looked lovely in their yellow gowns and white collars. The older teenagers and the adults who helped were standing on the sides and helped to sing. I gave a nod to the pianist and organist and we started our first song. "On a Night Like this, Anything could Happen". After just a few measures I noticed a young boy getting whiter and whiter. He stood in the second row. Seconds later I saw him projectile vomit! The product of this physiological happening came up and out onto the back of the singer in front of him. There was also some vomit down the front of the young singer. It came up and out silently so no one else was even aware that it had happened.

My thinking was to keep directing until the song was finished, then I would dismiss the young man. I could not catch the eye of the pianist, (the boy's mother) and she started to play the introduction of the second number. This number was about Mary and Joseph going down the street; Mary was on the donkey. The sound effects of the "clip-clop" was a special musical wood block. This instrument is played by the musician keeping in proper time with a mallet. To my utter amazement, the boy who had been sick reached to the floor, picked up the wood block and began to keep time with the music. I could not contain myself. Trying desperately to control my laughter, I tried to direct and mouth the words. As I would think about what happened grins came and I almost convulsed with laughter. The helpers were beginning to wonder what was wrong with "Mrs. D". I'd gain control and the next minute "joy would bubble". Those were the longest twenty minutes of my life.

We finished the little musical. I nodded for the young boy to go out first and go downstairs to the choir room. I told the one who stood in front to also go. The sick boy left, the second one stayed. I had instructed the singers that when they finished they were to go down into the sanctuary and sit on the front pews. The rest of the choir refused to go off the platform. Then one of them came in from a side door and handed me an armful of red roses.

They were lovingly presented to me and finally I could not hold back the chuckles. I attempted to say, "Thank you so much for these roses. I never before had roses like this." And then the dam broke! I uttered, "I'm sorry! One of our choir members up-chucked" and then I ran off the platform. My husband sat in the congregation wondering what ever happened to me. He never saw me so out-of-control! The congregation did not have a clue.

This writer will never forget the night that "anything could happen"! After it was all over we had a good laugh. Truly –"A merry heart doeth good like a medicine" (Proverbs 17:22)

DUKE the Dentist
CHAPTER 12

Almost everyone in our community knew him as Duke. I never did learn how he got his nickname but especially in baseball circles he was always "Duke" DeLancey. Very quick at short stop, he loved the game and played baseball all through his school years. Before we were married he wrote love letters to me and addressed me as "Duchess". I always thought that was so romantic.

He had his serious side, too. When he was twelve years old he was listening to a radio broadcast and the speaker was Rev. Percy Crawford. In the family living room, beside the old time radio, he saw himself as one who had sinned against God and he prayed and asked the Lord Jesus to be his Savior. As a young Christian, he didn't understand many of the Biblical doctrines but he did know that Jesus died for him.

All through high school

he had other activities along with sports. Loving music, he first played a mandolin, then a cornet in the high school orchestra. He never admitted it but he also had a lovely tenor voice. Diligent in his studies, he was readily accepted into college at Elizabethtown, Pennsylvania. His baseball career continued through college and he was always proud to tell us that his college team played Army at West Point.

Unfortunately he was born with a genetic condition that caused many cavities. One by one he lost his teeth. By the time he was nineteen he had a full upper denture. This interest in dental care grew to the extent that he decided he would like to become a dentist. He took the tests for dental school and especially passed the dexterity exams where the student was required to carve small models and show manual skills necessary for a dentist. Financially he was helped by receiving a Senatorial Scholarship. After receiving a BS in science he went off to Dental school.

One of his professors was very dogmatic. When Don wrote an exam he put the answers the professor wanted, but at the bottom he was convicted to write something like, "This is what the book says, but I don't believe in evolution." The professor answered, "What in the 'blankety blank' do you call this?" When Don saw the teacher's reply and continued to hear his profanity in class, he thought, "I can't sit under such a godless man any longer. What shall I do? I have a senatorial scholarship. Guess I'll never be a dentist." However, he wrote to the Senator and very soon he had a reply saying that it was no problem, he could transfer to another dental school. He applied at the University of Pittsburgh Dental School and was accepted with no questions. Did this just happen? It was God's providence to bring Don to Pittsburgh where we would meet two years later.

In the meantime back home in his home town of Sellersville, the town fathers knew that a home town man would be graduating from dental school and there was no dentist then in the community. They investigated and later found Don working as a graduate dentist at Pennhurst State School in Spring City, Pennsylvania. It was a special institution for mentally and physically challenged children and adults. Don was ministering to these needy folks and was saving money to start a private practice. We were able to start our married life together on that campus and were blessed with personal contacts with some of the residents.

The town fathers made a proposition to Don. "Would you come and be our dentist in town? We will remodel rooms on the second floor of the Odd Fellows Building and if you will serve us here we would rent out an office suite for you." What a blessing! With no hesitation we accepted the proposition and Don had a very busy dental practice there for thirty two years.

"Duke" loved his patients. Every morning he prayed at the breakfast table that he would know how to treat each one and that he would "charge the right price." Always active in sports he played tennis for most of his later years. Still a dedicated athlete, he won many tournaments. To play sports was a release of tension for him after doing precise dentistry most of the week.

In August of 1983 he advanced to the finals in the Pennsylvania Senior Games in tennis. During a final match, a storm approached and the referee saw Don staggering on the court; he had a hard time running. The match was called. Don was able to get to his dorm where he suffered a massive heart attack. Due to the quick thinking of his roommate who ran for medical help, he was revived with CPR and lived three more years. His second heart attack happened in our home in February of 1986. Again he responded to CPR which Dan, my son, and I performed. The medics were there in less than ten minutes and continued the resuscitation. He lived three more weeks until his heart surgery.

The night before surgery, he was being prepared and so we decided to leave for the hour and a half drive home. My mother was with me. I said good bye to him. As I left his bed and came to the door I called back to him and through the curtain said "Good night, honey." He replied, "Good night." I believe he knew, as I did, the possibility of not surviving. We both knew the gospel song:

"We'll say good night here and good morning up there." For Christians it is never good bye!

He went into surgery the next morning and never woke up. Three days later he passed into glory. Now I would be alone without a husband but never really alone. "Lo, I am with you always, even to the ends of the earth." (Matthew 28:20)

As I think about his home-going from time to time, I am reminded that he never had the privilege of seeing his seven grandchildren:

Brooke Nicole DeLancey
Adam David DeLancey
Caleb Joshua Trittipoe
Seth Thomas Trittipoe
Joel Donald DeLancey
Hannah Margaret DeLancey
Rachel Isabel DeLancey

When we all get to heaven, what a day of rejoicing that will be!

A SPECIAL DAD

I've lived with a dad for 34 years
   We've shared many things together
He's been by my side so faithfully
   In fair and stormy weather.

He's the father of our children
   A man of good report
Has convictions and there he stands
   Molded from the uncompromising sort.

So gentle and so kind
   His soft words so sincere
A careful, exact person
   Who loves his family dear.

I love my wonderful honey
   Who is balding and a beautiful grey
So distinguished is his carriage
   Many a heart he could sway.

But he's mine, all mine and precious
   God gave me this man you see
How I praise the Lord for this treasure
   A Christian husband for me!

- Margaret B. DeLancey

Happy Father's Day, honey!
June 1984

Summer of '86

Chapter 13

After Don's burial and memorial service, spring was a great adjustment period. Dan and John had graduated from college and were living at home, but our home was an empty place when they were at work. It was just Laddie the Second (our collie) and I roaming around from room to room. When I retired at night—the empty side of the bed made me realize that he was really gone. Thank you notes were written, some friends called, a few came to visit. My life was radically changed. Much time was spent collecting valuable documents and banking information for the lawyer. Unlike most widows, I had to sell a dental practice.

How was I ever to do this? What will happen to all our wonderful patients?

One young dentist was interested; Don had talked to him while he was in the hospital before his surgery. The dentist deliberated and decided not to step in but to stay where he was. So I called a fine Mennonite dentist who took over our calls when we were on vacation and he said, "Yes!" The agreement of sale included a clause that I would be in his office for sixty days as a liaison who would introduce our former patients to him. One day, as I was in the business office, the music over the radio system spoke to my heart. The love song touched me so much that I went to the restroom and shed a few tears. *My beloved husband was gone—oh how I miss him.*

I came back to my desk and tried to work. I wanted to be brave and not let my emotion show. Then the dam broke and I said that I needed to go home! I left crying and when I arrived at my home, there standing in the driveway was the same pastor who helped me when I went through the garage door! The dental assistant had called him and he came up the hill from a few houses away just to console me. That was such a blessing.

When I finished my sixty days, my faithful daughter called and suggested I go to their home in Virginia for a week—just to get away. Sounded good to me. She planned to come, we would have a garage sale, and then she would drive me in her car.

Our trip to Newport News, Virginia, turned out to be an exciting event. As we drove south on the interstate highway, the car coughed and sputtered. Rebekah got out, looked under the hood, but didn't see anything wrong. So we started off again and a few miles down the road she pulled off and stopped again. She had seen a flashing red light in her rear view mirror and thought she better obey the signal. A sheriff in full uniform ran to our car and ordered us to get out of the car immediately. "Your car is on fire!" He had been watching our car and saw flames shooting from underneath. "Run back to my car!" he exclaimed. He immediately radioed the fire company and the LORD had them practicing in a field just three miles away. They came almost instantly, got the hood open and put out the fire. A broken hose had wrapped itself around some wires. The car still started and she decided to "limp" to the nearest phone (no cell phones yet) and call her husband Gary about our next step. She ended up pushing the car when it finally died for good. We got through an intersection and then down a grade to a restaurant parking lot. Gary, being three and a half hours away, said that it was up to us for figure out what to do next.

As we talked at the restaurant counter, a young man heard our conversation and said that he knew a chicken farmer who had a truck. Maybe he would take us to Virginia. We called Gary again and he said he would pay the man if he brought us to their home. We were to leave the car there for future attention.

Mr. Smith (not his real name) soon appeared with his pick up. He emptied out the back the best he could. Chicken feathers still stuck to the floor! He agreed for a given price so we loaded our stuff. Suitcases, heirlooms, cameras, garment bags and our present valuables all got loaded into the back. Then we started to climb into the cab and the young man said. "Mr. Smith. I'd sho like to go along. I ain't seen the ocean for a long, long thi-mm." Mr. Smith agreed.

Rebekah and I looked at one another. Trusting that it was God's provision we got into the cab, Mr. Smith, Rebekah and I, and the young man—all lined up on the front seat. Off we went. We came to a tunnel and Mr. Smith said, "I can't go more than fifty with this truck and that big semi behind us is going to push us through! I believe I prayed almost every minute of that trip. *We don't even know these guys. It is two against two! What if they kidnap us? Rob us and leave us dead? Lord help us!*

Halfway across the twenty-six-mile bridge over the Chesapeake, they stopped at a rest stop. We whispered, "What if we go to the rest room and they drive off with all our stuff? Let's hurry and keep a watch." When we got back to the pick up they were there. Off we went and finally we were delivered into Gary's arms. He paid them, they returned to go north and we praised the LORD! This was in June 1986!

The end of this story was six months later when the chicken farmer bought the car. He planned to fix it himself. Gary and Rebekah were at church one Sunday morning and thieves broke into their house and stole the money!

July 4, 1986 was another exciting time. John decided to run a triathalon celebrating our country's birthday. The race started in New York as contestants swam around the Statue of Liberty. Then they biked from New York to Philadelphia. After this they ran a 10-k foot race to Independence Hall. His fiancé Sue and I went to watch the finish. Temperatures zoomed to one hundred degrees that day. We had lawn chairs, water, snacks, sun hats. Everyone cheered each runner as they passed and encouraged them to just keep going—they were almost done. We both saw John! "Look—he is limping! Even staggering?" The fans yelled and cheered. We watched as he crossed the finish line and fell right to the street. Medics came immediately. On quick examination they yelled, "Get his family—this one is going to the hospital!" *Lord, am I losing a son after I lost my husband? Did he have a heart attack?*

As I prayed for the Lord to help him, we quickly piled into the ambulance with all our stuff. They immediately started an IV and when we arrived at the Pennsylvania Hospital discovered that the ER was full of athletes and patients were lined up in the hallways. Nurses came from all the floors to take care of this emergency. John regained consciousness and the cramps in his legs began to subside. We were there for several hours. *Thank you Lord it was not a heart attack!*

When he was released, we had to go and find his bike. At the courtyard and all over the street runners were lying on egg crate mattresses. Family members were holding the IV's. It looked like a war zone, but the hospitals were full and they decided to do it this way. Perhaps the race should have been called because of the heat?

We arrived home at midnight and I praised the LORD that I didn't lose another loved one. John and Sue were married a month later.

The family had encouraged me to plan to go to Israel later that month. The Associates for Biblical Research were sponsoring another archaeological dig for the Biblical city of Ai under the supervision of Dr. David Livingston. They all agreed it would be good for me to "get away". So I packed and left with a group from Philadelphia, flying to Amsterdam and arriving in Tel Aviv. This was my third trip to Israel but still exciting for me. Every time you go to Israel you learn something new. (Just like every time you read the Bible, you discover a new truth). We settled in and the plan was for us to tour for three days before we started to dig. On the third day we were exploring Tel Azekah. Hiking to the top we gazed down at the Valley of Elah where David killed Goliath. After a fine lecture, we ventured back down the path. About ten feet from the bottom, I slipped on some loose gravel and fell, ending up in a sitting position. I looked down at my legs and my right foot was pointing out to the right, completely out of position. I told the man in back of me, "I think I broke my leg!"

"What did you say?" I repeated the fact that I thought I had a fracture and asked him to go and get Marilyn. She and I were to be the two nurses on the dig in case anyone got hurt! She ran to my side and agreed. She ordered the men to scout around in the brush and find something for a splint. I had ace bandages. We decided I should take a pain medication right away knowing that if I had to have surgery, I wouldn't drink again.

They carried me to the van. All the digging tools in the back were consolidated and room was made for me to prop up my leg. We stopped for ice but it was Shabbat and they could not open the freezer. So we used precious drinking water on the foot and ankle. I remember claiming Jeremiah 29: 11, "For I know the plans that I have for you, declares the LORD, plans for welfare and not for calamity to give you a future and a hope." The verse was clear in my mind because when Don went to glory a dear friend gave me that verse.

When we finally arrived back in Jerusalem we could not take the whole group to the hospital so we dropped them off at the study center. Those remaining—the guide, Dr. and Mrs. Livingston, and Marilyn the nurse stayed in the van and we stopped at the first hospital. They couldn't see me. They only had one doctor and he was in surgery. The second hospital accepted me. God provided again. The assistant to the doctor in the emergency room was from the USA and was doing her internship there in Israel. She spoke perfect English!

Then started the melodrama. Take to x-ray. Look at pictures. "Very bad. Very bad!" Tibia and fibula both fractured and foot out of position! The doctor decided on no surgery but closed reduction. I winced as he started the manipulation. Told me to relax my abdomen and to hold onto the railing! I replied that I was sorry and I was trying to be a good patient and that it was four hours since the time of injury. They gave me more Valium and Demerol. They put on a cast, took pictures and decided, "No good!" Cut the cast off, and put on a second one.

When I woke up they told me I would be staying over night upstairs! I had a new thing to carry around—a cast from my toes to my groin! Ever been in a hospital where they don't speak your language? A few did, and the physical therapists and a tall big head nurse showed me how to use crutches, even to how to go up and down their big steel steps.

My following days were spent in a wheelchair or on crutches. I had an emergency phone call that my brother Reuel had died at the age of 52 and of course I couldn't go home. The whole group was great and supportive—bringing me my breakfasts, helping me at meal times, and even sending me flowers.

Coming home on the plane I was taken to a special lift and put into the cabin of the plane and then my leg propped up with milk carton boxes. At home I continued with wheelchair and crutches, and then a smaller cast. But I was not allowed to walk until November. That was four months God gave me a rest from running all over the place! I learned so much in that time about how special friends and family were to me and how that Jesus was my best friend!

Indeed, I remember the summer of 1986. The LORD was teaching me many wonderful lessons! "Come unto me all ye who are weary and heavy laden and I will give you rest." (Matthew 11: 28)

"One Broken Leg"

Things just don't happen to the children of God
They are a part of His wonderful plan.
So why should I question the fact that I
Broke my leg in Jesus Land?

The day had been so successful
Hebron, Beersheba, and Lachish
But that is when my touring stopped
My climbing and studying ceased.

But that last climb had been so exciting
To the top of Tel Azekah
Where we viewed the Valley of Elah
Where David killed giant Goliath.

It was on that last almost level slope
Not rocky, but gravel so loose,
I just slipped and slid and then I looked
At my twisted crooked foot.

So close to the van and not high on the rocks
There I lay with all gathered around,
Brothers and sisters in Christ—so concerned
Making a splint as I lay on the ground

Some sacrificed and sat in the rear
To give me an outstretched seat,
Merilyn used cold, cold water
Which helped control swelling and heat.

Dave and Gene did the careful driving
Down dirt roads, and winding highways;
After three hours we came to Jerusalem
And from there sought medical aide.

The first hospital had no room
Reminds me of Mary and Joseph,
But the hospital that did take us in
Was the one God had chosen.

This hospital was on call that night
For the city of Jerusalem,
For orthopedic emergency cases
And I was one of them.

That certainly was of the LORD
With an ortho doctor there to care,
And a lady intern from Philadelphia
Who spoke English and was a dear.

But you know, Lord, in my inmost mind
I feel sorry for self and for pain,
Please teach me as I sit and wait
And give hope that I'll walk again

I'll try my best to ride out the storm
We've had many trials before,
I just pray that I will heal quickly
And in time walk in my own door.

I thank Thee for the prayers of people
Both here and way back home,
Who not knowing about my broken leg
Still pray "Thy will be done."

Through this may I learn many lessons
As I sit, and with crutches walk,
Teach me, Lord , and let me find
Chances for witness and Spirit-led talk.

I know I could choose to sit and cry
As I journey to my heavenly home,
Instead of moaning and asking "Why?"
Let me rest on Thee alone.

Margaret DeLancey July 16, 1986 Jerusalem, Israel

(Diagnosis—Fracture of right tibia, and fibula, and dislocated foot, was allowed to walk again—November—four months later.)

Riding the Rails
CHAPTER 14

I called my mother to give her the exciting news. She had two great-grandbabies, a girl and a boy named Brooke and Adam. "Would you like to go and see them?" I asked. She thought it was a wonderful idea. Plans were made to fly to California.

I drove to her home in western Pennsylvania and we flew to California from the Pittsburgh airport. Carol met us when we arrived and she was carrying two babies in carriers, one on each arm. Dave was still on duty with the Navy in the Middle East and arrived home weeks later. I am not sure how much help we gave to Carol especially when I blew up a bottle of formula in the microwave. Mother's brother, Uncle Frank, came from southern California with his wife to visit mother. They had a good reunion.

After two weeks of trying to help, we decided to rent a car and to go see a few of my friends. Dear friends Don and I had met on our first trip to Israel in 1980 invited us to visit them. After a good night's rest, we enjoyed a lovely breakfast; we planned to go to church together. Our host asked mother to pray. She started out and then slurred her speech, then she went unconscious. We quickly took her chair back and slid her onto the floor. Our host, a medical doctor, ran for his stethoscope and determined that it was her head and not her heart. Four emergency vehicles responded to our call and many medics handled the case.

In the ICU of the hospital, the doctors came to a decision that they had little hope that she would survive. They asked me to put her on a "No-code" which meant they would not resuscitate her. I felt that I could not do this because of my siblings back home. I called them and explained what had happened. My sister Roselaine was away camping with her family and the State Police had to find her. My brother Robert, Roselaine, Faith and the rest of the family concluded that if it has to be, we would leave her in the Lord's hands.

By ten o'clock that evening it was suggested that I go home and get some sleep. I went in to her cubicle to say "Good Night". She opened her eyes and I asked her if she knew me. She said clearly," You are Margaret Belle." I explained to her that she was in the hospital and that the doctors are caring for her. I also said we should get a little sleep and that I would be back in the morning.

I prayed with her, then rushed out to the nurses' station. I said, "Take off that NO CODE. Let's see what happens!"

She stabilized under some sedation and the doctors said she really needed surgery. One doctor didn't feel it wise to do it in California because she would have no family to help with the rehab. What was I to do?

She slept a lot and I waited from day to day. I found the name of a Baptist church in one section of a local newspaper. I called and the pastor came to visit. In fact, he came almost every day she was there. He would read scripture to her and sometimes she would finish the verse because she had memorized so much of the Bible. One day he read Philippians 4:13, "I can do all things through

Christ," and she said out loud, "Which strengtheneth me." Even though sedated, her subconscious mind remembered the precious verses.

My sister, Faith, also a nurse, decided to fly out and help me. We counseled with the doctors. They said we could not fly her home because of the air pressure. One alternative was for us to rent an RV and drive her all across the United States and medically monitor her as we traveled. The other plan would be to bring her back by train.

Off we went to the Travel Agency. We were told that the RV place was closed for the weekend. The agent also said she doubted we could get on the train but she would try. She called Chicago and would you believe, they told her there was one compartment left! We would have to get on at a whistle stop about a ten minute drive from the hospital.

What a miracle and what a scramble! Faith and I scooted off to the drug store and bought medical supplies. The hospital made all the final arrangements. The ambulance rushed her to the train station and we followed in a van. Over the loud speaker we could hear the announcement that the train would be stopping for seven minutes to pick up a little old man. We quickly said, "No, a little old lady!" The ambulance crew hustled mother up to the second floor of the train. Others helped with all our bags and supplies. Off we went, living for three and a half days on a train!

Through the desert, over the Rockies, into the Midwest plains, through farm country and then to Pittsburgh. We had to change trains in Chicago. This gave us a lay-over of a few hours. We arrived about lunch time so we bought some soup and some nourishment for Mother. Then we were told we could not take food into the lounge area. We appealed! She was a wheelchair patient and sedated; we needed to try and feed her. We won!

By then, we two sisters were swaying back and forth because of the train motion. Add to this extreme fatigue, we felt like two zombies. In Chicago, Faith had to sit on the floor while she talked on the phone. She thought she would fall because of her poor equilibrium!

By 6:30 AM on the third day, we arrived at the Pittsburgh station. What a joy it was to look out of the window and see family members waiting for us. The ambulance rushed Mother on to Presbyterian Hospital and after preliminary studies, surgery was performed to clip her aneurysm.

Three months of rehab followed. She came home to our family residence. Mother wanted to resume her violin lessons and that she did! We were so thankful that she recovered and enjoyed several more years with our families.

Riding the rails! It was worth it! Did we see much? Sometimes we saw the canyons, the mountain peaks, the farm lands. Much of the time we were busy with our patient. We all had a good laugh one day in our compartment when mother accidentally pulled the wrong chain and the shower opened up and poured over all three of us! In every instance the Lord went before us and directed our paths. We never dreamed He would take us all across America via Amtrak!

To God be the Glory!

New Assignments
CHAPTER 15

I was fifty-seven years old, soon to be fifty-eight, when Don graduated to heaven.

What will be the next step for me? Go back into nursing at a hospital? For the last twelve years of Don's dental practice, I've been his office nurse. Lord, what shall I do?

Dan and John had graduated from college and were living at home. I was keenly interested in missions and three months into my widowhood, I drove to the office of the Association of Baptists for World Evangelism in Cherry Hill, N.J., and had a conference with Dr. Wendell Kempton and Dr. Russ Ebersole. They listened and after a long conference said that it was too soon for me to decide. Dr. Kempton told me, "Go home and love your sons." This was such good advice.

A few months later my pastor saw me on a Sunday morning and asked me to consider coming back as Director of Music. You may remember that I had felt led to resign in 1983 and a short time later, my husband had his first heart attack. I had been in that post since the early seventies. The reason they needed someone now—the present director was having a baby! I prayed about it and in a few days said, "Yes, Lord!"

As months went by, I was thinking about Don's memorial service and was so glad that we decided to say "No flowers" at the memorial service. The only flowers we had were two lilies up front with a lovely poster standing between them. The poster read, "REJOICE WITH ME". An artist Robin Heller had made the sign for us. Don and I had gone to a memorial service where a small sign, saying the same thing, was right on the coffin of the deceased. The father, before he died, had told the family that he didn't want them to cry but to rejoice because he would be healed, no longer in any pain, he would see the LORD, and he knew that eventually he would see his wife and children because they had accepted the LORD as their Savior. So I elected to do the same thing. Instead of flowers I suggested that family and friends contribute to Don's memorial fund and we were able to send about $4000 to the Carolyn Kempton Christian Memorial Hospital in Togo, West Africa. As I contemplated all this, I started to have a keen desire to see this place where we might have served. Don and I had been in contact with Dr. David Clutts, the doctor who had supervised the building of the hospital and was in charge of services there. There was a dental chair and equipment sitting in a small room in the hospital. It could be a dental office. And they had no dentist. Don had asked the heart surgeon if he fixed Don's heart if he would be able to go to Africa and the doctor said he should be fine if all went well. The Lord had other plans and took Don home. The thought stayed with me—I would like to see the ministry in Togo!

One Sunday I casually mentioned my desire to Rosemary Bossard, RN. She said that she had been praying about doing something like this. So we planned and flew to Togo in January 1988. We had put out an appeal for a project, "Medicines for Togo" and worked with Merck, a drug company in New Jersey. They donated $6000 worth of drugs especially a specific drug for Africa's "river blindness". With private donations we were able to take medicines valued at about $10,000.

While in Togo, Dr. Bill Commons, from the ABWE office came to visit and encourage the missionaries. (Association of Baptists for World Evangelism) Dr. Commons spent time with me as I searched for the Lord's leading. While I was there, I had been asked to teach Creation subjects once a week in their chapel time at the MK school. (Missionary Kid School). I had never done this before. It was my husband who did the speaking on the subject. I did remember some of his lectures since I would accompany him if possible and sat on the back seats and listened. There were two creation books there in the small library of the MK school. So I asked the LORD for wisdom and with the Bible, those two books and my memory, gave them material that I hoped would reinforce the MKs when they went back to the states on furlough. Then the African lab technicians wanted to hear what we taught. I did three sessions with them using an interpreter. It was like God saying, "Margaret, this is what I want you to do." Dr. Commons suggested that I go to different mission fields and do the same thing there.

So when we arrived back home in March I began to study more. Phone calls started coming with invitations to come and speak. My willingness grew into seventeen years of ministry. In July of 1994 I was leaving the International Creation Conference in Pittsburgh. For a short cut, I walked across the soccer field of the university which hosted the conference.

As I walked towards my car, I heard the Lord saying to me, "What is in your hand?" "*My car keys!*" "What is in your hand?" He asked twice. Again, the third time, He asked me the same question and then I realized the answer, and said out loud "Creation Evangelism!" I had already been busy doing it, but the Lord seemed to want me to continue.

Invitations increased for me to teach Creation in churches, schools, camps, and home school groups. I also had another "hat" and was still Director of Music in my home church. I was told to plan all the music, and do the monthly schedules and when I wasn't there; there would be someone to take the leadership. However, I analyzed my last year when I had been absent for eighteen Sundays and I felt it was time to give up the music ministry so I finally resigned. Creation Evangelism was also taking me to various mission fields and I was becoming more and more burdened for missions.

"What is in your hand?" The Lord asked Moses the same thing in Exodus 4: 2. God gives all of us some sort of ministry. What is in your hand?

Missions in Togo, West Africa

CHAPTER 16

Togo is a small country located on the map as you "go around the hump" of western North Africa. We flew there via Amsterdam, Holland, and then south to the capital city of Lome. Our visit to Togo was a cultural shock. Everyone there spoke French or a tribal language. Of course we could communicate with the missionaries but not with the nationals. They smiled at me and sometimes bowed because they revered my white hair. (and age!) That year I was the oldest one on the hospital compound.

Electricity there was a premium. We only had it for twelve hours from 8:30 AM to 8:30 PM. In the evening we were warned five minutes ahead of time that it was time to shut down the generator and to light our oil lamps. Someone was assigned to strike the large bell that resounded through out the camp. Once the oil lamps were lit, the tiny insects made it through the screen and went for the lanterns. When we had too many gnats for comfort we turned off the lamps and used our flashlights and went to our beds.

My working days started at 7 AM. The national nurses and missionary staff helped me with communication. I realized the importance of really knowing the language if you were there full time. I usually worked on the wards but once in awhile in the operating room.

Sunday mornings the missionaries branched out to different local churches. My first experience was to go with Jane Schmitz to a church via mud and sandy roads. At one place we had to maneuver our car up and around a large hole of water and mud. We prayed that we wouldn't get stuck. Closer to the church we saw Togolese people walking from all directions and one mission van pulled up with an overload of people. We counted eighteen people on the van and the tires even looked flat!

That first Sunday I heard a message in French and only understood "Jesus Christ". As the service progressed I was aware of the fact that there was a great wind stirring outside of the frame building. I could see through the opening of the wall and the roof that there were severe gusts of wind. Dust was flying and also the few trees were bending dangerously. I watched with frightened eyes thinking that maybe it was a tornado-like storm. As quickly as it started it stopped. I was wondering if it was some kind of a Satanic attack? I saw the fervency of the missionary and how two men responded to the Gospel. For me it was a great initiation day for me, observing a real missionary at work on a real mission field.

Every missionary has to take supplies that will last for four years. This is multiplied of course if you have a spouse and children. Since we were "short termers" we were asked to bring with us certain supplies like soap, toilet paper, toothpaste and other personal articles. It was a big discovery the first morning there when I fixed my instant oatmeal. Close to the oatmeal we had packed some Irish Spring soap and the oatmeal enroute had picked up the scent and all of the oatmeal tasted just like Irish Spring! I didn't want to throw out the oatmeal so I tried to adapt to the soapy taste. Experience is a great teacher.

We were there over the Easter season. Some of the missionaries had taken their musical instruments to the field but rarely used them. Since I was teaching the MKs and working with them, we decided to have a special Palm Sunday musical evening and we invited the whole Field Council to participate. This meant that the adults would be a part of our program. Two of the doctors retrieved their trombone and trumpet from storage. Another missionary played the flute. We practiced special songs and we found that one of the OR nurses had a fine tenor voice. So we had him sing the first part of the "Holy City" and then all thirty-three of us came in with "Jerusalem, Jerusalem, Lift up your gates and sing!" Yes—we did the Holy City as one of our special numbers! We all enjoyed the fellowship and worship time together.

One of the special numbers was performed by the one who played a flute. She was to play through a hymn and then we were to sing the rest of the hymn along with her and the pianist. At the precise time, a swarm of gnats came through the screen and attacked the soloist. She stopped and swatted at the insects. Then she tried to catch up to the pianist who had not seen what was happening. The soloist stopped and swatted again. They were swarming about her face and neck. By this time our whole solemn bunch of missionaries were snickering and laughing, as was yours truly, the director. Somehow we composed ourselves and were able to finish the hymn without the flute. The insects gave us much joy in worship and it was a memorable time because we did a whole hour of music, honoring our Lord.

There were no street lights on the compound! One requirement for us was to bring flashlights and batteries. We were instructed to use them when we went to an evening meeting or to the hospital. We needed to keep our path lit in case there was a poisonous snake in our way. Hopefully we would avoid stepping on one. While I was there I only saw one snake and that was a blessing!

Climate-wise we were there during Harmatan. This is when the dust from the Sahara Desert blows in the air and settled on the furniture and all surfaces. It affected the air so much that by 4 PM it just got very dark. We found out that because we were close to the equator that there are no sunsets or sunrises. It just gets dark and then gets light. Temperatures can rise to well over 100 degrees. So overhead fans were great while we had electricity.

When we got to the rainy season and temperatures got to the seventies, the missionaries were freezing. Rosemary and I thought the 70's were great! Rosemary, by the way, was led of the Lord to go back and serve there for a year as a nurse. So she did have her share of hot weather.

I saw the dedication of the missionaries as they presented the Gospel of our Lord Jesus Christ and then saw how people were changed. It was impressive to see the churches that were established by the missionaries and the new converts. I have been ever so grateful to be able to visit Togo and then to go back the second time. One day I was sent to a patient in the ward to take his blood pressure. I reached for the man's hand and there was no hand. It was a shock to me. I didn't know that he was a leper and that he had lost his forearm. He was there to have just a simple cataract operation. That one experience alone made me realize the medical need in countries like this. These missionaries had answered the call and I saw them in action. My visits to Togo made me burdened to pray for our missionaries there and around the world. I was also challenged to be a missionary right where I was planted and to speak boldly of my faith in the Lord Jesus Christ.

Acts 1: 8 - "But ye shall receive power after that the Holy Ghost is come upon you; and ye shall be witnesses unto me both in Jerusalem, and in all Judaea, and in Samaria, and unto the uttermost part of the earth."

Mikafu Mawu

Komi was a thirteen-year-old Togolese boy. He dove into shallow water two weeks before we arrived in Togo, West Africa. The doctors diagnosed him with a fractured cervical vertebrae and consequently was confined on a fracture frame. Komi was a complete quadriplegic. I could not communicate with him and sometimes I saw the tears trickle down his face. A sweet six-year-old sister was there often to help feed him.

One day the sister brought a round ball of baked dough wrapped in a green leaf. I pretended that I might take a bite. We communicated with our eyes and he learned to call me "Grandma-ma". He was strapped to a bed and for four hours at a time he would lie down with his face toward the floor. What boredom. A missionary gave us a lovely decorated paper plate with scripture written in French across the face of the plate. We placed the picture on the cement floor so that when he was upside down and looking down he could see the picture. We observed a smile on his face because we got down and looked

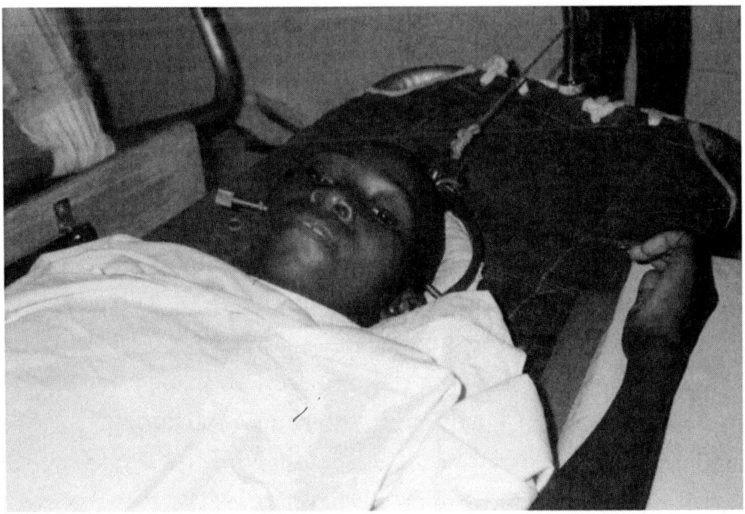

up at him underneath his special bed! We also found a picture of Jesus so for four hours he was able to look at something different than a plain surface. Some of the staff became interested and brought a variety of pages to entertain him.

The national workers in the ward were wonderful because they could talk to him in his language. They told him all about Jesus and what He did for us when he died on the cross. Komi understood and told them that he wanted to believe in Jesus. From then on, Komi had a radiance and hope in his eyes. He knew he was loved! The workers continued to teach him Bible lessons. What a change of countenance on his face! Jesus lived there now.

The missionary doctor said that he would probably go home to the village to die. No where in Togo is there a rehab center. Because of inevitable infection from bed sores, from pneumonia, or just lack of care, he could die even in three months! The sadness of this was dispelled by the fact that he would eventually be healed! When he departs from this short life here, he will have everlasting life and a new body! "Mikafu Mawu"! In Komi's Ewe language this means—"Praise God!"

Every day we spent time patterning him as we exercised his arms and legs. We took each arm and each leg and attempted to train his movements. One day we decided to put a life saver in his hand. We exercised him and showed how he could put the candy into his mouth. With help from us, he did it, and he smiled because he liked the taste! So we worked with him and little by little he was able to get his hand closer and closer. Then one day, he made it and got the life saver to his mouth. He was happy and we shouted for joy. We continued working with him several hours each day, but sadly the time came for me to say good bye. Our days of patterning him came to an end and I had to leave to return to the USA. His big smile was an encouragement to me as I left his bedside with tears in my eyes.

Two months later a report came to me from Togo that Komi had left the hospital! He was able to fully use his arms. He was able to feed himself and manipulate a wheelchair. He went home a radiant Christian. Now I am looking forward to a special day when I meet him in heaven!

MIKAFU MAWU!

A Long Tiring Day

We had been on duty since seven o'clock in the morning. The clock on the wall said 8:30 PM. The day had stretched out long and demanding. Dr. Cropsey had just lifted out a limp baby from the Togolese mother via C-section. The baby didn't cry. He handed it over to my friend Nurse Ann.

Ann was a very wonderful and caring nurse who was in charge so I watched with amazement as she began to work on the baby. She quickly inserted a small catheter into the baby's air passage and began to suck out mucus. When she got some into her mouth, she got rid of it and started again. This is what you do when you don't have sophisticated equipment. She tried again and again. Suck, remove, spit, insert and repeat. Then after many mouth-to-mouth tries she picked up the baby by its feet and spanked its bottom. All at once, the baby howled! We were elated! The baby stabilized, the mother's abdomen was closed, and mother and baby were sent out into the women's ward.

By this time we were starving. Well, not really, but it had been a long day and we didn't remember when we last ate. We had to clean up the OR before we left in case there would be another case during the night. I lived in the same missionary house as Ann, so we went home for a 10:00 PM supper. French toast never tasted so good!

This was a very special day for me. The excitement of seeing a limp baby come to life, seeing a dedicated doctor and nurse at work, finding out that as the day goes so God gives strength.

As I reviewed this episode I am thankful that as of this writing there has been a whole separate wing added to the hospital and now the ladies have their own special maternity ward and delivery room. But there is a reason that this particular experience was such a blessing. I remembered delivering my four children and how I had medical care and caring doctors and nurses.. The above happened on a very special day. I was far removed from my children who were thousands of miles away across the ocean.

It was Mothers Day celebrated in Togo, West Africa!

Roses in Heaven?

Chapter 17

Once a month in our church we had a special musical evening. Members of the congregation entered a request for their favorite hymn. The program was planned to accommodate the requests. Individuals as well as the choir presented a program that we always enjoyed. My husband requested a song, "Where the Roses Never Fade". As director of music, I had to compile the program and told him, "Honey, I am not sure it is scriptural and I never heard of the song." He strongly replied, "Well, that is my request—period!" Since I wanted to honor my very own husband, I researched and did find the song in a southern gospel song book. The choir sang it and he was pleased.

Three years after he went to glory, I was assigned to clean out the dental office in the mission hospital in Togo, West Africa. You may have remembered that my husband had wanted to sell his dental practice and go there as a missionary dentist. I emptied the cabinet drawers, washed the instruments, scrubbed the dental chair and as I worked I realized that this equipment was not being used; no dentist serving here. Suddenly I was very sad. It was our wedding anniversary that week and his birthday was coming later in the month. The tears started and then flowed. My heart ached. Then, I looked out the window and saw a large bush with beautiful red flowers. Not really roses, but the flowers made me think of the lyrics, "I am going to a city where the roses never fade". *Maybe there are roses in heaven and he is enjoying them?*

I attended the yearly missions' conference that summer and was asked to give a report on what it was like to be a short term missionary in a country like Togo. I mentioned the red flower incident. After the session was over, two of the leaders came to me and said the song was a fine song and they would sing it for me. Would I be there for the closing program on Saturday morning? Needless to say, as they sang, the tears flowed again. I am so glad they warned me about singing. I was prepared with my Kleenex!

Several years later as I was traveling for the Creation Evangelism Ministry, I left the interstate in northern North Carolina to find a family I was to visit. I got lost and had no idea where to go next. I saw a church up ahead and a pick up truck sitting alone in the parking lot. I pulled along side and addressed the driver, asking him about the road that I was seeking. He asked me the name of the family I hoped to visit. Immediately he answered and gave me great directions to their very house. He was the rural mailman! I marveled how the LORD was still directing me even though I thought that I was lost. Thanking the postman and the LORD, I drove carefully out of the parking lot, turned on the radio and over the air waves came, "I am going to the city where the roses never fade". God was also comforting my heart. "Even though you thought you were lost I am still with you. Your hubby is here with me where the roses still bloom!"

I had not heard the song again until October 2007. I went to a memorial service for a dear servant in our church. The vocalists sang a duet and it was her favorite song. My son Dan was visiting me at the time and he held my hand while I listened and cried.

As I heard it again I thought of heaven and how beautiful it must be. We do read a great verse in I Corinthians the second chapter, verse 9, "But as it is written, Eye hath not seen, nor ear heard, neither have entered into the heart of man, the things which God hath prepared for them that love him." He is preparing mansions for us. Some kind of a dwelling. It seems so reasonable that there will be flowers there along with the tree of life which will bare twelve manner of fruits. God created the beautiful rose here on this earth. Surely he will prepare much of this beauty in our heavenly home, where the roses never fade, nor the bush dies. What a day of rejoicing that will be! We will meet the Creator!

"Where the Roses Never Fade"

I am going to a city. Where the streets with gold are laid
Where the tree of life is blooming
And the roses never fade.

Here they bloom but for a season,
Soon their beauty is decayed
I am going to a city. Where the roses never fade.

In this world we have our troubles
Satan's snares we must evade:
We'll be free from all temptations
Where the roses never fade.

Loved ones gone to be with Jesus,
In their robes of white arrayed,
Now are waiting for my coming.
Where the roses never fade.

E.J. and J. Elsie, Jack and Jim

Around the World in Eighty Days?
CHAPTER 18

Never! That is, if you are traveling with Dr. and Mrs. Joseph Stowell Sr. You will do it in a month! Why would eighteen of us go on such a whirlwind trip? Our purpose was to visit many missionaries who are serving under the Association of Baptists for World Evangelism. We hoped to encourage them. To not go was to miss an opportunity of a lifetime! Visiting dedicated missionaries in many countries was a challenge and an inspiration to each of us.

Merging together in San Francisco we had to wait a day because our plane needed repairs. On March 28, 1989, we left and arrived in Manila. Because we had been delayed, the student body of 160 students was sitting for almost four hours to hear our leader speak. As we entered the campus of the Baptist Bible Seminary and Institute, we heard them all cheer. They were patiently waiting and we as travelers were so tired, but we were blessed in worship and in the teaching of the Word by Dr. Stowell.

We flew to Iloilo the next day and again saw the fruits of our missionary efforts. We participated in the graduation of 218 students of the Doane Baptist Bible Institute which was founded in 1923. Of the five hundred churches in the Philippines at that time, all but one pastor graduated from Doane.

Back in Manila, we were entertained by the missionaries there as they sponsored an "American Pie Party." Such a treat was readily accepted since we had been exposed to many Asian menus. It was a joy to see Dave and Becky Nelson, second-generation missionaries. We also met Dr. and Mrs. Ken Cole who, being medical people, decided to make medicine secondary and evangelism and church planting their first priority.

Then we flew to Papua New Guinea. With no main highways from city to city, we used small transport planes from place to place. We saw PNG from the ground and from the air. Village after village, there are people who are open to the gospel and want missionaries to come. When they hear about the good news of Jesus dying for them, many of them shout and dance for joy! One group of believers in the Duokonage Church prepared a Mu-Mu-feast for us. The food was cooked on fires in the ground and then served on banana leaves. We ate with our fingers!

One special afternoon we traveled on a dirt road to a village called Kamusi. It sat on top of a mountain at the 7,000 ft. elevation. We started up the dirt road to the top and discovered that the rain had left the road very muddy. All at once the van, full of people started to tilt dangerously and was about to turn over on its side. The missionary who was driving ordered us to carefully get up slowly, and not jump or move fast, and one by one leave the van. The mission was accomplished. Then the missionary had to work to get the van out of the mud and he moved ahead once he accomplished his task. As we walked to the van, one by one we slipped in the mud almost falling. We finally climbed back into the van midst the noise of great laughter! When we arrived at the top of the mountain believers were waiting to show us their church. We sat on boards for pews.

We heard a message in their language. This group of people had seen another Christian tribe and observed how kind and loving they acted. So they built a church first and then prayed that God would send a missionary to tell them about Jesus! People in Papua New Guinea had never seen white people until World War II. Before this many tribes were cannibals and ate people. How the gospel can change lives!

In Hong Kong, we spent four days. One of the days we went to the China Baptist Theological College. Young believers are trained to become pastors and to be taught in the scriptures. We had tea from real China tea cups and ate food with chopsticks. I never became too adept with them, but managed. For those of us who struggled, they brought us an "American" fork! Churches have been established in Hong Kong and there are daughter and grand daughter churches, some of which we visited. The missionaries have established some senior centers where the participants hear the gospel. Another very fruitful ministry is the establishment of Christian schools, especially of the kindergarten age. How precious the children looked in their little uniforms.

One day we took a boat and went to China. As we disembarked we saw large ponds where the Chinese farm fish. We walked on the narrow path between the ponds and I was really frightened when coming toward me was a water buffalo. There was no room for both of us and I backed up and let him pass. Otherwise, I would have had a swim with the fish! We learned a little bit about Chinese medicine and their special teas.

Our next country was Thailand. We flew into Bangkok and were met by missionaries there. It was a very hot day when we arrived and we traveled in taxis through very narrow and dirty streets. We came to a store front and all got out and saw the sign- "Grace Baptist Church". It was like a beacon of light in a world of darkness. Entering, we found a full church! Shining, happy Christians singing like you have never heard before. We were lifted up and we were encouraged. That particular day they prayed for one of our missionaries and a national who planned to leave after the service and go to the border to try to see the national's parents. They did this with the possibility that they could be shot, but we learned later that their mission was accomplished even though the missionary became very ill. They celebrated that day the fact that twenty-five years before the Philippine Association of Baptists for World Evangelism started to send missionaries to Thailand. It was a day of celebration for all of us! By their fruits ye shall know them!

Bangladesh was our next stop. It was an impoverished country ravaged by floods seven months before, and now by drought. After we left they had tornados. Highlight was to fly into Chittagong where a gang tried to rock and upset our bus because they wanted money. The authorities rescued us, and we continued on. Another blessing was to travel by vans over a one lane road for three hours in order to see the Memorial Christian Hospital, founded by Dr. Viggo Olsen. The staff was anxiously awaiting the arrival of my friends Dr. and Mrs. Lincoln Nelson. This devoted "retired" couple, were coming to Bangladesh to relieve the medical staff there for several months.

Our final visit was London, England, where we only stayed for one full day. Then we crossed the great Atlantic pond and arrived in New York. Yes—around the world—covering 25, 992 air miles, and many more miles by boat or highways. We were in sixteen different planes and had nineteen take offs and thankfully nineteen landings! Truly it was a fantastic experience. The fields are white unto harvest! Pray that the LORD will send forth laborers.

Another Super Happening!

In one of our flights when we traveled around the world I met an interesting lady. Flight plan was to fly from Manila to

Hong Kong. We were in line for the restroom—were to land shortly. This lady in front of me was friendly and we engaged in an interesting conversation. Her husband was a pastor and chose to stay home for his local responsibilities. She was with a small group of people who were visiting missionaries a week at a time. They did special jobs, like repairing equipment, painting, assisting in ministry. They hoped to be an encouragement to the different families. She said she was having a glorious time. What a delight it was to talk to her.

Three days later, I saw her again! We were on a boat, skimming over the water, headed for Macao, China. We were so surprised to meet a second time and continued our new friendship. I discovered that she lived in the same area of Pennsylvania where my sisters lived. In a few months I planned to visit my mother near there and stay for a week. I promised my new friend that I would call her when I was in her area. Midweek of my stay with my mother, she called me! "How did you know this phone number?" I asked.

She replied, "My mother-in-law goes to a card party every Tuesday evening. As the ladies talked she learned from my sister's mother-in-law that I was in town." I thought that this was quite a coincidence. Then she continued, "My mother-in-law is Belva Jean Sinn—your father's second cousin!" I even remembered Belva Jean when I was growing up in our little borough. She was in high school and we grade school girls always looked up to the girls who were older than us.

I know what you are saying to yourself as you read this! "Small world"! Truly it is, but I say that meeting a distant relative half way around the world and seeing her a second time was a very special and exciting event. I call it a "God thing"!

Visits with Rev. Ed Bomm
Chapter 19

I met Rev. Ed Bomm at a Missionary enrichment conference of the Association of Baptists for World Evangelism. My friend Rosemary and I chose a seat at a long table and I ended up sitting beside this man of God. I had traveled around the world with Dr. and Mrs. Joseph Stowell and spent several days in the Philippines. Mr. Bomm was so excited to know that I had been there because he served many years as a missionary in that same country. He and his wife were also prisoners of war under the Japanese and they had written a book about their imprisonment entitled *Beyond Prison Walls*. So we had much to share concerning the Philippines.

As I became acquainted with him I discovered that when folks went to visit this tall white haired man of God, they would go home richer than when they went. Although they came to cheer and encourage him in the faith, they always left uplifted by his faith, wise counsel and insight.

His first recorded visit in our home was September 8, 1989. How do I remember? He signed our guest book. Our family more or less adopted him and often during the holiday seasons he would join us for family meals. He introduced to us the idea of singing after we prayed. He usually asked us to sing the "Doxology".

During his last several years Mr. Bomm had encounters with pneumonia, cancer surgery, and heart problems. Many of my visits took place in the hospital. What an encouragement he was to us even in sickness. Often when he was so ill he would close his eyes and his lips would move in prayer. How he loved the LORD!

As his physical body failed more, he longed to go home. A week before he went to glory, special friends from New Jersey came to visit him. As they left, one of them said, "If we don't see you down here, we'll see you up there!" We saw his face brighten with joy! Frequently as I left his bedside I would say, "I'll see you here or there or in the air." Again he would smile at the thought of going home to heaven.

Mr. Bomm was a praying man. Our visits always included prayer. When I prayed for him, he would add a prayer for me and my safety. I lost a faithful prayer warrior!

Mr. Bomm truly hid God's Word in his heart. Often when we visited together he would ask for his "daily vitamin" which was a reading from the Bible. Two days before he died, we chose Psalm 23. As I read, he recited the chapter with me. The next day we read Psalm 1. Every time I deliberately stopped, he would fill in the word. After I finished reading Psalm 1, he repeated verse 4 which says, "The ungodly are not so, but are like the chaff which the wind driveth away." Even in his final days he was concerned for those who have never accepted the Lord as their Savior. He said before I left that day that he liked Psalm 2 as well. He was so exhausted and I told him that we would save that Psalm for tomorrow. He smiled and agreed, then closed his eyes. He heard me pray and he prayed. That was my last visit with him. Tomorrow never came for us! He slipped away the next morning before I arrived at the hospital. Our friend for almost eight years was gone.

In his last week he said that he thought it was his time to go. I told him that he couldn't go until the LORD was ready for him and sent his angels to carry him away. The doctor told me that in the emergency room, in his last hours, he kept saying, even with shortness of breath, "I want to go home!" The LORD heard his plea and took him to Himself. What a joy that must be! I have often wondered if they sing the Doxology in heaven?

One of Mr. Bomm's last visitors was his friend Mr. Bill Pearson. When I came later that day I asked him, "How was Mr. Pearson and what did he say?" In a childlike manner he looked at me and said, "He told me that he loved me." I replied, "Everyone loves you, Ed!" He left this world, leaving many friends.

One day the redeemed of the LORD will worship around the throne. I know that we will be forever with the Lord! We will have an eternity for visits!

Rev. Edward C. Bomm July 27, 1902- June 15, 1997

JAPANESE PRISONER

You have just read about visits with Mr. Bomm. You may recall that he had been a prisoner of war under the Japanese for three years. Since my family appreciated Mr. Bomm and my son Dan was living in Charleston, South Carolina, I decided to take Mr. Bomm to see Dan. He had his lonely moments and I thought this would be an encouraging thing to do for Dan. After a few short days of visit, we left to drive home.

Late in the afternoon we stopped at the "Golden Arches" for a rest stop. To eat healthy we took our bag of fruit with us and planned to buy a milkshake. As we entered the restaurant the bag broke and the contents rolled all over the floor. We scrambled to pick up the apples and oranges and another couple also helped. We were all laughing at the comedy of it all. When we caught our breath Mr. Bomm asked the couple, "If you would die tonight where would you be going?" I knew that he had a way of witnessing, so I excused myself and went to the restroom. When I came back they were in a startling conversation! This very lady had lived in Manila. Her parents were teachers, and since they were American citizens they were also imprisoned. She was only six years of age at the time but remembered vividly the prison camp and the surroundings. As they compared notes they realized they had been together at the same time in the Santa Tomas Prison in Manila, Philippine Islands.

The man with her was her son, a student in medical school. He and I listened as they shared story after story of their internment. Mr. Bomm told how, for a birthday celebration, they cooked a cat for their dinner. She was so excited and asked if they could sit with us? Stories of their imprisonment were shared for over an hour!

I stayed in touch with this lady for two years and then lost contact when my last letter was returned to me. We marveled later about the timing when a broken grocery bag made it all happen. Mr. Bomm and I thanked the Lord for this encounter!

Surprise at a Banquet

Another time I took Mr. Bomm to a banquet which was celebrating a Christian ministry. We had assigned tables. Mr. Bomm, gentleman that he was, introduced us to the other folks at the table. Each gave their names. Then I added that Mr. Bomm had been a prisoner of war in Manila and that he and his wife had published a book about their experiences.* One lady

---

* Book—*Beyond Prison Walls*, Published by Association of Baptists for World Evangelism, PO Box 8585, Harrisburg, PA 17105-8585.

directly across from us commented that her brother enlisted in the Army. He thought that he was going to Europe, but was sent to the Philippines. "It was the best thing that ever happened to him," she exclaimed. As she continued we learned that when her brother, when he was in Manila, attended the GI Gospel Hour programs and met some wonderful Christian leaders. He heard the messages and promised to serve the Lord. When he came home he became a pastor and served in a church in New Jersey. She concluded with the fact that the leader of the GI group was Rev. Ed Bomm.

We gasped! She had not really heard his name on the introductions. Mr. Bomm and his wife, when they were released from prison, had started this wonderful ministry to the American military now stationed there. I replied to her, "This is Mr. Bomm!"

The lady was ecstatic! As the two of them exchanged more information Mr. Bomm said that he really did remember her brother and had the privilege of attending his ordination service in New Jersey,

Are you saying, "Small world?"

Short and Tall

One evening I took Mr. Bomm to see a Bob Jones Christian movie in a local church. We arrived a little early and a very short in stature usher came to welcome us. Mr. Bomm was a very tall man and as he bent down to shake hands, we all exchanged greetings. The usher asked us about our own churches and I interjected that Mr. Bomm had been a missionary in the Philippines and was stationed in Manila. This had been about fifty-five years ago. The usher then commented that when he was in Manila in the military that he attended the GI Gospel Hour center and that he had learned so much from a Rev. Ed

Bomm. Can you imagine the shock and surprise when Mr. Bomm said in his deep voice, "I am Mr. Bomm!" What a picture it was to see this short man with tears running down his face, reaching up and hugging Mr. Bomm. We again marveled at God's providence and His surprises!

Now, isn't God good?

The Attic
Chapter 20

An attic can be a fascinating place. Memories came quickly when I entered my attic. Suitcases and travel bags reminded me of many lands, special people. Boxes of yarn and already crocheted granny squares waited patiently on the "to be finished list". Backpacks, remnants of by-gone hiking days, hung on the far wall. Old lamps and unused curtains were stored on the floor underneath the backpacks. One quarter of the attic housed the Christmas decorations. An artificial tree about three feet tall stayed decorated from year to year and hid under a plastic sheet until it was time to shine. A rocking horse stood silent for over thirty years. Yes, my attic was a friendly place but very ominous if you couldn't get out!

Right in the center of the attic was an old cedar chest, a family heirloom, and some boxes where I kept extra sheets and bedding. I entered the attic to get some fresh sheets. It was a very cold day, and I closed the door behind me so the cold air would not enter the small hall and my upstairs bedroom. Mission accomplished, I turned to go back and make my bed. The door was locked! *No problem. I will find a nail and put it into the little hole in the lock and I will spring it open.*

I spied a tripod that we would use on the cemetery—the kind that holds flowers. *That should work!* I poked the one prong into the key hole. It would not open! Viewing other possibilities, I found a larger tripod. *This will really do it!* Nothing happened. I tried and tried to no avail. I wasn't strong enough to break down the door.

How long can I stay up here? There are plenty of blankets to keep me warm. Should I scream? No one would hear me with the carpenters using saws and pounding nails on the house they were building across the street. Who, if anyone, would miss me? I could be up here for days, and there is no food or water. I could stay warm, but starve to death. Maybe the two ladies I am to pick up for the missionary meeting tonight might investigate, but that is ten hours away. Is there any way to get out of here?

In the far end of the attic there was a small four-foot door. I had to stoop down to go over the garage. There we had loose boards across the rafters so we could store roof shingles, sleds, empty barrels and some wood. I lowered myself through the door and walked gingerly on the boards. I could see my red Pontiac through the open rafters on the side. *Maybe I could get down somehow to the top of my car? How would I do that?*

I crawled back to the attic proper and there I spied an old clothesline wrapped up from the ceiling. *How long ago was this clothesline used? Is it rotten? Would it hold me? Is it strong enough? Maybe, if it is still a good line, I could take it out to the garage, tie it around my waist and jump. I sat down on the dirty boards with my legs dangling through the opening on the rafters. Hmm… Maybe that won't work? If I jump and miss the car, I would hang by the rope until some one found me.*

I removed the rope from my waist and decided to place the rope around both wrists. Then, if I jumped, and landed on the car, I would be stabilized from falling off the car onto the cement floor. *Lord, I'm scared! Joshua was afraid, too. You told him to be strong and of good courage. Give me courage and here I go!*

I jumped and landed in the middle of the car roof. The roof was bent in! After untying the ropes from around my wrists, I slid down the windshield and jumped off the hood to the garage floor. Then I looked down at the six-inch gash on my left leg. I must have hit the metal garage door box on the way down. With gratefulness and praise, but still shaking, I went into the house and dressed the bleeding wound. As I cleaned up and got ready for the day's activities, I was so thankful for family and friends who continually prayed for me. I was also thankful that the roof of the car popped back up and didn't need repair.

You can believe me that the lock was changed so that would never happen again. My attic, now under new ownership, still gives me one more memory—that of deliverance and praise.

Joshua 1:9 - "Have not I commanded thee? Be strong and of good courage; be not dismayed. For the Lord, thy GOD is with thee withersoever thou goest." I learned that lesson well on December 11, 1990.

In the Beginning—God!

Chapter 21

"Let me get this straight! So, this is what you are saying? Billions of years ago there was a great explosion of four elements? Hydrogen, ammonia gas, methane gas and water vapor. From that explosion of a very tiny particle, small enough to fit on the head of a pin, we got our magnificent universe? Now I wonder, where did you get those elements? Where were they hiding if there was nothing, absolutely nothing, before this big explosion?

You continue to teach that after this tremendous explosion the earth was formed? Your books say that the earth was very hot and had to cool down. Then it rained on the earth for millions of years. Where did we get the rain?

How did the water come to be? It is made up of two gases—hydrogen and oxygen. What held these two elements together to make even one molecule? How did it come to pass that there were enough molecules to cover the earth completely with water?

Then you tell me that at one point there was lightning and it struck the water somewhere down on this earth. When it hit the water, a living cell was made. How can that be when lightning is so powerful? It is usually 3-4 miles long, five times hotter than the sun, and contains 15 million volts of electricity.

Real science tells us that lightning burns and destroys. And you say that it made the first organism?

You also teach that the first cell multiplied and made another cell. Did the cell grow? Did it take on nourishment? Even if there were just two cells, they would have been the only living things in the water. When did they start to eat or did they just keep multiplying? At one point in this cycle when did they make an organism? You tell me that eventually they got together and made a fish! What did the fish get first? Did it get its vertebrate first? If so, it needed to have flesh and muscles to hold the bones together. It needed a tail to direct its path through the water. The fins had to be there to give it balance. If it had a stomach, it needed a mouth to bring in the food. It seems to me that that fish had to have all its parts in place in order to survive as a fish.

And when did plant life begin? Did it also come from that first little cell? What determined that a cell would be a plant cell or an animal cell? And when would there be enough cells to make an organism? Was plant life growing also at the same time? What did the plant life grow into?

So how long do you think it was before those fish started to grow legs and start climbing out of the water? What fish were elected to do this? I ask because there are still millions of fish living in our vast bodies of water. Some have not changed.

You say the fish that grew legs climbed out of the water and became reptiles. From the reptiles we got all our land animals. You even teach that some reptiles turned into birds. So we can look at a family tree of one simple little cell and see from that beginning we have camels, roses, cows, tulips, palm trees, lizards, giraffes, cactus, monkeys, and finally people! So how do you explain that every living thing has its own design, its own DNA? Is your process observable in real science today? Does this evolution really happen?

In real science, everything produces after their kind. Elephants have elephants, not baby tigers. Cows have calves and not little cats. Big dogs have dogs and some dogs are smaller but they never have rabbits. Each one has offspring in their own family. So, I am sorry that I disagree with you about the origin of life. There might be a variation in size or color within a family of animals- but never a cross over from one kind to another. I would like to tell you I believe that in the beginning, God created the heavens and the earth and everything after its kind. A scientific study of every living organism shows the intricate design of a Creator."

The above conversation took place one Saturday afternoon with a young man who was taught in college the theory of evolution. It is still a theory and has not been tested otherwise. So that is why God kept me busy for seventeen years of my life traveling and teaching children, young people, and adults. The Lord opened up amazing doors for me as I traveled to twenty-six different states and ten countries, sharing my convictions. I was invited to teach in Christian schools, camps, retreats, churches, home school settings, and even in two large Christian School Conventions on the east coast. In those seventeen years

of creation teaching, attendance records say that "we" taught over 26,000 folks. God opened many doors of ministry. How great is our God!

Genesis 1:1 - "In the beginning God created the heaven and the earth."

Isaiah 45: 12 - "I have made the earth, and created man upon it: I, even my hands, have stretched out the heavens and all their host have I commanded."

Isaiah 42: 5 - "Thus saith God, the Lord, he that created the heavens and stretched them out, he that spread forth the earth, and that which cometh out of it; he that giveth breath to the people upon it, and spirit to them that walk therein."

Fly to the Windward Islands?

Chapter 22

It was not that simple! Buy a ticket and plan to go? It wasn't easy. Let's go back to November 15, 1994, when my correspondence began with Dr. Rolen Cornelius, director of the Harbor Light Radio Station on the Island of Carriacou. He invited me to come to the island to teach Biblical and scientific Creationism. He suggested that I do some broadcasting and with fear I said that I had never done that. His plan was for me to come and also teach on three other islands. Many months and many letters later, I was to go and depart on January 9, 1996.

But God intervenes sometimes with delays or cancellations. The day before I was to fly, our Philadelphia area had a thirty-one inch blizzard. Snow was piled halfway up my back door. I could get out through the garage and though dubious about being able to leave, had all my bags packed. A slide projector had to go with my carry-on. My monkey and dinosaur puppets, some fossils, slides, a wooden giraffe, text books and other teaching tools had to be packed along with my clothes. Then the phone call came from Pilgrim Travel that my flight had to be cancelled. The option left for me was to reschedule or take a refund. If I rescheduled there was no guarantee when I would leave.

The airport was closed for three days and if I arrived at the airport, I too could be sleeping on the floor with a pillow and a blanket. I called my pastor and he said he thought the Lord did not want me to go. Although on the surface I was disappointed, the Lord gave me deep peace that this is what I was to do. Take the refund.

Meanwhile my five-year-old grandson, Joel, was scheduled for his first of two heart surgeries. The other grandparents were to go there for the first surgery and I for the second. Because of the snow they were not able to go, so I was now free to fly the following week to Minnesota. The Lord knew all the time where he wanted me. A thirty-one inch snow storm sent me in the opposite direction and into contrasting weather. In Minnesota one day we had 40-50 degrees below zero.

Correspondence continued with Dr. Cornelius. My year was full and scheduled with meetings and camp ministry. "Let's aim for 1997!" And so we prayed to that end. Passage was purchased to go to the Islands in March of 1997. On January 14, Dr. Cornelius wrote about how they anticipated my coming.

It was just six days before my departure that a message from an area missionary was left on my answering machine. I learned that the man who invited me had gone home to be with the Lord. I sat in shock! This dear man had died at the age of 63. February 7 was a glorious day for him because Dr. Cornelius, affectionately called "Papa C", went to his bedroom to take a nap. God reached down and took him right to heaven. News concerning this never reached me.

After sitting in silence for some minutes, I called Carriacou and two phone calls later, I realized that I was still to go; they were expecting me. Providential? The Lord planned this. He knew about my interest in widows here at home. I was expected to stay with his wife, Arlene, now a new widow. So I continued to pack.

Four days before I was to leave, I developed cellulitis of my nose! Talk about Rudolph the Red Nose Reindeer, I almost had him beat. My wonderfully kind family doctor saw me in the middle of a busy Monday afternoon and prescribed medicine. This episode almost made me cancel the trip. Prayer partners said to just go ahead. The swelling extended from the tip of my nose up to my eyes but I reasoned that no one would know me even though I looked strange. So I boarded the first of two planes and safely arrived in Grenada, the first island. (Yes, my nose gradually got better!)

In Grenada I was assigned to stay in the home of a seminary graduate who trains and equips nationals in Christian service. His wife, a nurse, and their two boys were a delight to know. Ministry there involved speaking twenty-two times in eight schools and four churches and two Bible studies. We reached 1,775 students and adults. Eight came to me inquiring to know more about Jesus and how to be saved.

The next island was Carriacou. The Lord continued to bless with openings in government schools where we freely presented Special Creation by God. "Mama" C as every one called Arlene Cornelius was my hostess and we had great fellowship. She showed me much love and we traveled together through-out the island. She picked up folks for special meetings at the radio station. There always seemed to be room for one more in the van! Creation wise, I was able to reach hundreds in a youth rally. I also spoke in two prayer meeting groups, in a week day meeting of women, and taught some sessions with home schoolers. Several days I worked in the radio station taping five sessions of "Little Visits with Mrs. D".

St.Vincent was the third island. Dwight and Grace West (Baptist Mid Missions) were my hosts. I arrived in the evening and Dwight kindly helped me with my bags and got me settled into one of the dormitories. When he left, I thought I heard ocean. The next morning, to my delight, I looked out and my place was on a cliff, overlooking the Caribbean! We were asked to do at least twenty sessions in churches, small groups and in the Bible Institute. For those from the First Baptist Church in Perkasie, you may remember that Bob and Roberta Texter served there for two years in the Bible Institute.

The fourth and last island was the island of Dominica (not Dominican Republic). On the first plane all the seats were taken, so I was assigned to sit with the pilot! We cruised along and I watched the islands and the ocean below me. All of a sudden there was a loud noise and we flew right into a rain storm. The noise was deafening! You couldn't hear each other talk. After several frightening moments, we flew out of it and into bright sunshine. Tony and Martha Cornelius hosted me and there were seventeen opportunities to teach in the ten days I was there. Thirty-one children came to me and prayed the sinner's prayer. Only God knows the sincerity of their hearts. It was on this island that one teacher was thrilled to have someone come and teach. He had been listening to programs by the Institute for Creation Research and was very well informed.

Since the time I left on March 6, we had the fantastic opportunity to lecture seventy-three times. It was the prayers of God's people that sustained me through tight schedules, extreme heat some days, driving on bad roads, new situations in each school. I had wonderful freedom to teach in the government schools; in fact, they welcomed me and showed me great respect. I attributed it to the fact that I had white hair! I also had academic freedom, something we don't find in our American school system today. In one school there were at least three hundred uniformed children standing at attention the whole time I was teaching. The school didn't have enough seats for the whole body of students.

A verse that challenged me on trips like this was 1 Chronicles 28: 20 -"And David said to Solomon his son, Be strong and of good courage, and do it; fear not, nor be dismayed: for the Lord God, even my God, will be with thee. He will not fail thee, nor forsake thee until thou hast finished all the work for the service of the Lord."

Pola

Chapter 23

On Tuesday, January 21, 1997, I went by taxi from the missionary guest house to the airport in Manila. This was my last leg of a missions trip to Papua New Guinea. The Lord sent along a Filipino boy who helped me all the way to the check-in. I boarded the plane and had an uneventful flight over the Pacific. In Vancouver, British Colombia, after our first eleven hours, we were asked to deplane. The company planned to clean the airplane. It would take an hour. I walked around and after getting some needed exercise, I went to a row of seats in a waiting room area. A lovely lady approached me and asked if she could sit beside me. At first I thought she was a flight attendant. Trim and nicely dressed, she sported an attractive scarf around her neck. When she removed her dark glasses she asked if I was frightened when I saw her face. She had little freckle-like scabs as a result of surgery in Manila. I thought she still looked fine in spite of the temporary markings. She was Filipino, lived in Australia, and had flown to Manila to visit relatives. She had this special facial skin surgery in a clinic there. She was about in her fifth day post-op. She had been seated right behind me on the plane and she had noticed me coming and going as I got up for walking breaks. I had not noticed her until we talked.

Her destination was the same as mine. We fly all the way to Newark, New Jersey.

I asked about her plans. She was planning to get a motel for four or five days, rest up and heal. Then she would go to see her niece in the Bronx, New York City. This was her first time in America. *Hmmn. How lonely will she be in a motel in New Jersey?*

Somehow I blurted out, "I have three empty bedrooms at my house. Maybe you would like to come along home and stay with me? Think about it." The plane took off, and we settled down for our last leg across the United States.

What did I just say to her? She is a complete stranger. You don't even know her background. I live alone. What about my safety? Don often felt I was impetuous; he always took time to think things through. Should I have invited her like that? Did you think first, Margaret? Lord, please help me to know your will!

I settled down for a nap. I was in a row with three seats and no one there but me, so I took the blanket and got comfortable and took a nice rest. As we approached the airport, I still felt it was the right thing for me to do—the Lord seemed to tell me to continue my invitation.

As we landed and passengers prepared to deplane I asked her what she had decided to do. She said that she would come with me!

Now I am wondering if we will be able to take our entire luggage. One of our wonderful deacons often took me to the airport and came to pick me up and maybe he couldn't take us both? He only had a small car.

When I introduced Ray to Pola, he confirmed the fact that he certainly had enough room. After a two and a half hour drive to our small town, we settled in for the night. I gave her the front guest room on the first floor. I was back up in my own bed upstairs. I committed the night to the Lord and went sound asleep.

The next morning Pola heard me and came out to the kitchen. I was fixing some breakfast for us. After breakfast I told her that I usually read a little devotional book, read a passage in the Bible, then prayed to ask the Lord's direction for the activities of the day.

"Would you like to join me, Pola?"

She said that would be fine. Then we had to go and buy some groceries and fresh food items. That evening I taught another Creation lesson which was part of a ten-week course at our church. I had been given a two week reprieve so I could do the mission trip. This was a review and catch up lesson. Everyone in the class was friendly and she seemed to feel right at home.

The second morning came and again, I was in the kitchen. When I asked Pola how she slept, she told me that she did not sleep. She was up until just about two hours ago when she finally took a pill. She reported that she walked all through the first floor, back and forth for hours. Had been restless. When she saw a Bible on her dresser, she opened it and read some pages. Then she walked again until she could sleep.

We ate breakfast and then I asked her if she would like to do what we did yesterday. She affirmed, "Oh, Yes!" Before I read, the Lord prompted me to say, "Pola, I wasn't always a Christian. Just because I was born in America doesn't make me a Christian." Then I gave her my testimony how I had asked the Lord to save me before we were married. I told her that maybe she would want to do that some day.

She leaned right over the table and said, "I would like to do that right now!" I just about fell off the chair. I gulped and asked her if she wanted me to help her pray. She said, "No, I want to pray myself." She prayed the sinner's prayer and asked the Lord to save her! Then she told me, "This is what I have been searching for. I have been looking for peace and joy in many things. We belong to the country club. I took up ball room dancing, many sports, and nothing really has satisfied me." As we did more errands throughout that day, we met some of my friends and she would impulsively tell them, "I am a Christian now!" I marveled at her confidence and testimony.

On Friday of that week I took her to a bus terminal where she got a bus to New York City. After she visited with her relatives she decided to come back and stay a full week with me so she could attend our church. That was so special. She went on a day trip with our senior saints. As we rode along in the church van, we started to sing choruses and hymns. I couldn't believe that she knew those songs.

I asked her, "Pola, how do you know all those words and melodies?" She told me that when she was a teenager, she attended the First Baptist Church in Manila. She went to all the Bible studies and socials. However, she rejected the LORD and never asked Him to be her Savior. Again, I was astonished. That is the very church where Rev. Ed Bomm and his wife did the early missionary work starting back in the 1930's. She heard the gospel, but did not accept the free gift then. But—the seed was planted. This confirmed my conviction about reaching children and young people for the Lord. We never know when the seed will grow, if it will lay dormant, or flourish. Our job is to " go into all the world and preach the gospel". This assignment starts at home and reaches to the far corners of the earth. We are called to be witnesses and the Lord will give the increase.

At the end of her visit with me, her relatives drove from New York City to take her to her next destination. She eventually returned to her home in Australia.

This experience was a real lesson for me. How many times have I not responded to the prompting of the Holy Spirit and have lost a blessing of listening and obeying. This was one time I obeyed and it bore fruit.

It happened by God's marvelous Grace!

So, I went to Alaska!

Chapter 24

In the fall of 1999 I was invited to speak at a radio rally in Wisconsin. The next day, one of the radio announcers invited me to their home for dinner after church. I accepted the invitation with the stipulation that I could leave and not stay and visit. It would be much easier for me to drive through Chicago on a Sunday afternoon than to stay around until Monday morning. As we were eating, the host leaned over and asked, "Mrs. D., what is your schedule in the future?" I replied that I had an invitation to go to Alaska and was praying about the possibility. Immediately his wife excused herself, left the table, and went into a back room. She came back with a special prayer card. Her brother was a missionary pilot in Alaska. When I looked at the card I was shocked! Alaska is a tremendously large state, even three times bigger than Texas, and her brother was stationed at the Kako Retreat Center, exactly where I was invited to go. That was exciting news and confirmed to me that I should continue with my plans to minister there.

I flew to Anchorage, was met by another bush pilot. He took me to the home of a lovely couple. This was to be my headquarters during my stay in Anchorage. However, I had to first teach a Creation conference for a teachers' retreat at Kako in western Alaska. The bush pilot planned to fly me there, but the weather closed in and I had to go on a commercial flight to Bethel. The plane was half cargo and half passenger. We arrived at a very small airport and the waiting room was no bigger than my living and dining rooms at home. The Eskimos and Indians all scattered and I stood alone looking around to see only one man behind a small desk. I asked about my connection to Kako and with a phone call, he confirmed that my pilot was on his way. To be sure, it was Mark, the brother of my hostess back in Wisconsin. He looked at me and asked if I had boots. I rummaged through my luggage and found a pair of boots which I exchanged for a pair of dress shoes. We waded through the mud to the small Cessna and the adventure started!

It was close to nine in the evening when we landed on the small runway but it was still very light. The sky didn't really get dark until close to midnight. My luggage was dumped into a cart and was delivered later. We walked through the mud to the director's house where Vera, the director's wife had a hot meal for us. Steaming stew and home made bread!

Mark was my pilot the following week after the teachers' conference. Every day we would leave around four in the afternoon to go to a different village. We visited other missionaries, or taught Creation classes. I had memorized Psalm 121 back home before I came and each time we left the ground and climbed, I said it to myself "that the LORD would preserve our goings out and our comings in from this time forth and even forever more."

We flew over vast areas of tundra and frozen lakes. I learned later that the week before I arrived that Mark and another man had crashed onto a frozen lake. They had some scratches, nothing serious, but had totaled their plane because of engine trouble. I was so glad that I didn't know this at the beginning of my ministry there.

After my stay in western Alaska, I had to get back to Anchorage. Another pilot flew me through the Merrill Pass over absolute wilderness. We flew between the mountain ranges with peaks on either side. With head phones on to cut the noise we communicated back and forth. He said that it was the smoothest trip he had ever flown through that area. He usually encountered turbulent wind currents between the high mountains on either side. Again I thought of Psalm 121 and asked him if I could quote it for him. When I finished he said, "That is a blessing. That is what I have been studying and I plan to preach on that Psalm tomorrow morning!"

Psalm 121:1 – "I will left up mine eyes unto the hills, from whence cometh my help. My help cometh from the Lord, which made heaven and earth."

We landed safely and he took me back to my hosts who were leaving shortly for a concert at their church. When I heard "concert" I indicated I would like to go. They thought that I might be too tired, but were delighted to take me. The concert artist was a lovely young woman, a harpist. To begin her concert she played, "Be Thou My Vision" which was another thing my SS teacher back home had asked us to memorize. It was so exciting to see the hand prints of God many times!

I taught in several schools in Anchorage and was privileged to attend a Native American meeting that is held once a month. These Eskimos and Indians meet to share testimonies and to sing. I sat toward the back and the announcer said that, "After the next song, we will have Mrs. Margaret DeLancey come and give us her greetings." Gulp! *Did I hear right? How did they know I was here? What shall I say? Lord help me!*

While they did another special number, I prayed hard. In two minutes I was up front bringing them greetings from Pennsylvania and telling them that, "In the beginning God created the heavens and the earth." I don't remember what all I said, but they told me later that they taped it and that it would be on a television news cast.

I spent a week in Juneau, the capital of Alaska, with wonderful Christian friends, Rev. and Mrs. Johnny Reimer. I spoke in two churches there, then flew to the Kenai to be with friends Mark and Suzanne Weigner.

Departure after six wonderful weeks was from Anchorage. I had a "red-eye" flight which got me to St Louis in the morning. From there I flew to Philadelphia. I looked out of the window as we landed on the tarmac and prayed, asking the Lord to help me with my bags. The deacon who planned to pick me up at the airport said that I should be out at the curb. I was wondering how I could handle this myself.

I stood to deplane and started walking to the door. Ahead of me was a line of people. As I looked ahead I saw the back of one of the men and thought he looked unique, just the way he walked. When I got to the door I said to the flight attendants, "Nice flight!" and scooted out into the tunnel. I kept watching this one particular man and losing all inhibitions, I yelled, "Dave!" The man turned around and he said, "Mom! Were you on this airplane?" We were both in shock. "Where were you sitting?" he asked. "Row 21," I replied. Dave said that he had been in row 19. And we didn't know it. He was then a Captain for TWA Airlines and was flying back to Philadelphia as a passenger, but had no clue when I would be returning home from Alaska. The Lord provided me a baggage handler!

When I relayed this story to one of my friends, he said, "That is one in a million that a mother and a son would be on the same airplane and not know it. In our Christian life God does give us many surprises. Are you rejoicing with me?

One Sunday in Israel
Chapter 25

How many times has God protected me? Unseen times when we could have lost our lives in an instant? Other times we realized it was a very close call. We will never know because our days are numbered. Only the Lord does the counting. As I contemplated this thought I suddenly remembered one special Sunday in Israel.

An Egyptian, Arab, Christian missionary and his wife took me one Sunday afternoon to their church in Bethlehem. We had a day off from our digging and relished a day away from dirt and shovels. I taught Arab children in their Sunday School class. Yes, I used a translator. We were supposed to leave after the church service to go back to my group at the settlement. But first, I was told, we had to go to a party.

There was a young Arab man in their church who just got out of jail six months before. He became a Christian and was now announcing his engagement to a young lady in their church. In their culture, this demanded a celebration.

We parked the van at the bottom of a hill. From there I looked up and there was a path winding up past many small houses. We started our walking. It was very dark, no street lights. I kept thinking that I didn't want to fall and break my leg like I had done one time when I was here in this country.

Little did I know that the missionary had paid some small children to guard our vehicle while we were gone. We were in an area of civil unrest. We snaked our way up from one level to another. Finally we arrived close to the top and entered a modest Palestinian home.

Greeted in kind fashion we were all seated in a large circle and given a very sweet fruit drink. An Arab man sat next to me on the left. He just smiled at me, but we could not communicate. He was the father of the groom-to-be, and was so glad that we came. The missionary sat across from us and he said that I should know that the man next to me was the shepherd boy, Muhammed, who found the Dead Sea Scrolls back in 1945. He found the first of the jars in 1945 and kept them for two years in his tent before he showed them to his uncle. The uncle in turn showed them to an antique dealer and the rest is history. My heart raced! With an interpreter we communicated. Then Muhammed excused himself and went to the back room and brought out a small collection of some antiquities that he was still finding as he roamed through some local ancient ruins every weekend. I shivered with excitement. Am I dreaming? Then I looked down at my watch and knew we had to leave. We excused ourselves politely and left, seeking our way back down the steep hillside.

Fear began to enter my mind as I knew I HAD TO BE BACK at the settlement. The hour was really getting late! We made our way carefully and reached the van. It was intact and the children were still there with hands outstretched for more coins.

Back to the highway, we drove west to hopefully find our dig settlement. For this dig we lived right with the Jewish community who claimed they were from the tribe of Benjamin. We were digging for the Old Testament city of Ai. The missionary had a general idea of where to go. The missionary wife had me sit in the front passenger seat and she insisted on sitting in the back. I thought I remembered the way and we took a turn off to the left. The evening was so eerie! Not one car on the road! Not even a pedestrian! It seemed strange. We took the turn off I suggested and ended on a desolate street. There was one man up ahead so we stopped and asked him for directions. The man stared at us, an Egyptian Arab and a white American asking about a Jewish settlement!

His eyes flared. Anger was boiling in his being. "Quick! Quick!" we heard from the back seat. Obedient to his wife the missionary put the car in reverse and we sped away. Whew! We made it! He was certainly the wrong man to ask.

Back on the highway, still no cars. We traveled along and then slowed down when we saw a road block ahead. We stopped as two Israeli soldiers approached our vehicle. They came to our door, we lowered the window. Then the interrogation began. I asked if they spoke English. I told them I was an American and that my friends were taking me back to my archaeology group who was expecting me. I told them where we were digging. He was aware of the project. He talked to the other soldier and returned to tell us they decided to give us a military escort. I couldn't believe what I was hearing.

He told us to follow the two jeeps which pulled up in front of us. We started out and I immediately began to recognize some landmarks. They led us to the gate of the settlement and I got out after we were interrogated by the gate keeper. I was permitted to stay; my two friends had to leave immediately. The gate keeper took me in his car back to the community building where our group was staying. Seven of the twenty-two were waiting up for me. They were frantic and anxiously quizzed me of my whereabouts. They informed me that a curfew had been declared all over the region that evening. No one was allowed out of their homes. No cars were allowed on the streets or highways. We obviously never knew that!

My fellow-diggers continued to tell me that Israel had declared war games that evening! So I gave them my report. I told them where I had been and that I had met the shepherd boy who was now a middle aged man. They were shocked! We all praised the Lord! I was back in the fold! And, I was safe and sound.

I walked back to the open door in the large gym where some of us single girls bunked on army cots. The fellow diggers who didn't wait up for me were sound asleep. Quietly I got ready for bed, slipped under the covers and was almost too excited to sleep. It was dazzling to think how God had protected me and even used the Israeli army to do it!

This is the rest of my story:

The following weekend our group prepared to come home. We were back in Jerusalem packed to leave. The same missionaries wanted to take me to get a falafel sandwich at lunch time. My group leader said it was no problem. It would be fine; the bus was not leaving until 1:30 PM,

We went up a hill from the hotel to a little shop and ordered our lunch. All at once we heard a loud commotion outside the shop door. We ran to see. A man with a bull horn was outside yelling, "Everyone inside! No one on the streets!" We were forced back in. We prayed! I was wondering how I could ever get back down the hill to the bus? We tried to eat. The sandwich was no longer appealing. My stomach churned.

After thirty or more minutes we heard more noise. A siren was blowing. We ran to the door. We were told "All Clear!" Immediately we left the shop and started down the hill. I began to run. I knew I needed to get to the bus. The missionary lady said in her broken English, "Margaret! Don't run! They'll shoot!" I guess I was a "sitting duck"! A white haired American lady! She took me by the arm and made me stride with her. Her husband followed.

We arrived to the bus just in time. The bus went through Jerusalem and started downhill towards Tel Aviv. All at once the bus stopped. Someone had put oil all over the highway and the alert bus driver was able to stop the bus before we slid. One car before us had just hit the oil and crashed. After two hours of police investigation and road maintenance men spreading sand all over the highway, we cautiously advanced. Was it an act of terrorism?

We arrived at the Tel Aviv airport and safely flew home to the USA. The next day the rumblings of the Gulf War started and we praised the Lord for deliverance and His protection

Psalm 91:11 - "For He shall give his angels charge over thee to keep thee in all thy ways."

More Protections

Chapter 26

As I pondered many evident protections I began to think of my children and asked them to relate to me some of their happenings. These are their testimonies.

Dave, my oldest, is a Captain in the Navy and Navy Reserves. He initially flew A-7's, single seat fighter planes. He has had dozens of protections. He lost his navigation and radio equipment when his base in California was totally fogged in. He was saved by his commander who flew back up in the air to find him. During training in a formation drill he was pushed to 10 feet above the desert floor when the plane to the left closed in. He was the 5th and lowest of 5 planes in the formation. In a similar situation in the Indian Ocean, as the 13th of 13 planes in formation at night, he actually touched and bounced off of the water, pulled straight up, and ultimately lost the rest of the group, having to find his way back to the carrier alone. He has landed on various darkened aircraft carriers over 150 times at night, 560 times overall.

On land while out running on a trail, a large tree limb, big enough to crush him, fell to the ground inches behind him.

But his greatest vivid protection was when he was flying a Navy DC-9 with 38 Navy SEALs on board. Returning from a combat mission further west, they were flying the final leg from Manila to Guam. After waiting out several nights to avoid three Pacific typhoons, he was finally told by the official weather forecasters that the storms were gone. He and his crew lifted off for their destination in Guam.

The weather forecasters were wrong. During the flight, one of the typhoons did a 200 mile U-turn that placed it squarely over the island. As he approached the military air base on Guam his plane was overcome by severe winds and torrents of rain that allowed zero visibility. The military base is on the top of a three hundred foot high cliff above the sea. If he was too low he would crash right into it. He made two passes in the severe turbulence and rainfall, saw nothing outside the window, and decided to not try landing there.

He asked permission to land on the civilian airfield, the only other major airport on the island. Permission was granted. The rain and wind were unrelenting. He tried again and again, still no visibility. The tower asked how many souls were on board. If the plane crashed or ditched they would know how many were lost. On the seventh try there was a slight and momentary window of vision. There was not enough fuel for another pass.

He broke through the rain at full speed and, in crosswinds three times the legal and demonstrated limits, somehow landed on the runway. Full silence prevailed. Crew and SEALs sat in awe. They had considered themselves dead for the last hour and a half.

He eventually taxied forward to a gate and stopped. Since he was at a civilian airport, a Customs agent wanted to inspect the aircraft. You can imagine that SEAL cargo is not particularly suitable for a Customs inspection. With an incredulous look and tone of voice, Dave told the Customs agent to leave. He did. Just then the last of the fuel burned out and the plane went black.

Thirteen aircraft, with the same weather forecast, started for Guam that night. Twelve of them could carry enough fuel to divert elsewhere. They all diverted but the Navy DC-9 could not. Against all odds Dave and the SEALs made it. The winds destroyed the DC-9 on the ground later that night. But that's another story. I call that God!

From Rebekah:

Planes and Prayer

I was tired from a busy couple of weeks working away from home. All I wanted to do was walk through the front door and crawl into my own bed. But first, a string of flights had to be endured, Lynchburg, Virginia, not being the hub of domestic travel.

After hours of rain delays, my fellow passengers and I climbed aboard a small commuter plane. Wheels up, I was lulled to sleep by the drone of the engines and the darkened cabin. However, as the announcement of a final approach was made, I awoke and peered out my window. Expecting to see lights below, I saw nothing but white. Had it not been for blinking lights at the tip of the wings, I would not have known they were there. Still, we approached the airfield from the south for the landing. As we descended, the pilot spoke into the microphone. "Folks, we will not be able to land due to heavy fog. But, we think we may be able to approach from the north and duck in under the fog cover just in time."

So up and around we went to repeat the process. But this time it was different. Our descent was steep and crazy. Still, no sight of the ground. Though it may have been a single instant, I remember looking around the cabin to see passengers clutching their seats. I glanced at my watch. Something was wrong and everyone sensed it. It registered that we were going to crash. Knowing Gary was waiting for me in the terminal I clearly thought, "I wonder if he'll see the initial explosion. I guess my Mom will see this on the national news. I hope she takes the news okay." Somehow, I was calm.

Suddenly and without warning, the nose of our plane was jerked into an ascending position just as I glimpsed a runway light a few feet below us. There was an audible gasp as we were flung heavenward in a maneuver not unlike than Mr. Toad's Wild Ride at the amusement park. Dead silence followed for a few minutes, finally broken by the shaken pilot's voice announcing we were headed south to land in a neighboring fog-free state. His faltering words confirmed the close call. But that's not the end of the story. Two days later my father-in-law called on the phone. "Beck, I need to tell you something." He was hesitant and uneasy. I knew it was something serious. He began to describe how he was lying in bed, arms crossed over his chest. He suddenly awoke in a cold sweat. His heart raced and screaming through his brain was but one thought: "Pray for Becky."

And pray he did, if not frantically. "Keep Becky safe, Lord. Keep Becky safe." And just as suddenly as the prompt to prayer came, it stopped. He once again felt calm and reassured, drifting back to sleep without understanding what had just happened.

As we spoke I asked him what time this had occurred. You guessed it. The exact time I glanced at my watch as we were hurtling toward the ground. Did my father-in-law's prayer keep us from crashing? Was his obedience to the Spirit's prompting the element that saved us? I don't know. But I'm glad he prayed.

I may never understand the role of our prayers in the implementation of God's will. But I do know that when the Spirit says pray, we best obey.

Ground Hog Day

When I asked Dan about how God had protected him he assured me that God always has watched over him especially on his Honda motorcycle. One year he was able to drive from Pennsylvania all the way to California and back. He pulled a trailer behind him and that alone made him even more cautious. God even provided when he realized on the Ohio interstate that he had forgotten to bring a pillow. As he drove along the flat highway, he saw something on the shoulder of the other side of the road. He was able to turn around and investigate. There lay a clean white almost new bed pillow. He was so thankful God had provided just what he needed.

But God was even so evident on a warm, seventy degrees Tuesday morning in April of 2006. The balmy weather predicted a beautiful bike ride back to South Carolina. We prayed that the Lord would protect him and send his angels before, with, and behind as he traveled those seven hundred miles.

That evening he called me about 9:30 PM and reported that he was in a nice motel near Fredericksburg, Virginia. I wondered to myself why he didn't go any further. We exchanged "I love you" and the conversation was very short. The following evening he called again and reported that he was home. Then I heard the rest of the story. He had not wanted me to worry about his situation the day before.

As Dan drove the first day on Interstate 95, going about 70miles an hour, out of no where came a big fat ground hog! He could not avoid hitting it. Remembering what to do if you would hit an animal, he pulled back as hard as he could, kept the bike upright and continued. A state policeman who saw what happened gave Dan a "thumbs up" for a good job and kept going. As Dan continued he noticed a wobble in his front wheel. There was mechanical trouble. Safely, he entered a wide shoulder of the highway and waited for help. He prayed and asked the Lord, "How will we get through this situation?"

Very soon a biker came along and stopped. They determined that some bearings were broken; the bike was not fit to drive. The biker suggested he call a dealer in town and they would come out and get him. Before the biker left, Dan, sensing he might be a Christian, came right out and asked him. The gentleman replied, "Yes sir! Jesus Christ is my Savior!" Then the Good Samaritan left the scene.

The truck came to take Dan and the bike into town. As they surveyed the damages, the Good Samaritan came back to see how Dan was faring. No repairs could be made that evening so Dan's new friend said, "We have a men's fellowship every Tuesday evening. Why don't you join us? "Dan was delighted and became a part of the group of men who were "one in Christ". They went to eat and then took Dan to a motel. The next morning another man from the group came and took Dan back to the dealership. Necessary repairs were made and by noon he was on his way again. He realized that God had kept him from crashing on a busy interstate and possibly being killed by a speeding car. God also provided help when he needed it and used willing Christian men to be His servants who helped another believer in the Lord!

Wild Attack Dogs

John, my youngest and twin brother to Dan, studied in Israel for one year. This was his third year of college as a Bible Major. He and a fellow student decided to take a day off and go to Jericho and climb up the back of the Mount of Temptation. This site overlooks the Dead Sea and was one of King Herod's fortresses. It is now a military base.

They enjoyed their hike but as they climbed the sun started to go down and twilight settled in. John and his buddy decided to just go to the very top and descend the front side of the mountain. Halfway down the mountain is a monastery. Plan A was to hike down to the monastery and ask the priests to let them go down the front steps and the path below to the road. Knock, knock. No one came. They knocked again- no response. They needed a new plan.

They decided to go back up to the top and hike down the back in the dark. They couldn't find the trail. What should they do? They stopped and prayed for guidance. Suddenly they heard the barking of dogs.

The dogs approached the hikers and in response the hikers quickly started to run. Israel is known for their wild and vicious dogs and these were moving in a pack chasing the young men. They ran and ran! The dogs savagely chased them. The runners finally came to a stop. The dogs had given up and the men stood there alone on the side of the mountain.

They caught their breath and analyzed their surroundings. As they scanned the area they were astonished that right before them was the path they had hoped to find earlier. Proceeding cautiously they retreated down the mountain. When they reached the base they spoke with an Israeli soldier who was kind enough to call one of John's professors. He came with his car and drove them back to Jerusalem.

God used dogs! God answers prayers!

The Year - 2001
CHAPTER 27

Pack and unpack. That had been the routine for fifteen years, but the Lord began to slow me down. In January I had a routine and yearly mammogram. Four days later I was called back for a retake. The suspicious x-ray revealed an early breast cancer. Surgery was scheduled and my spring meetings were cancelled. Radiation therapy followed for six and a half weeks.

By summer I was able to resume my schedule and travel. I drove to northern Michigan and taught for two weeks at Camp Gitchee Gumee. Back home in our home church another teacher and I supervised a real archaeological dig on our church property.

This supplemented the classes I taught on Biblical Archaeology. Can you believe the excitement of the children? They just loved digging in the dirt, finding objects, washing rocks, making sure their square was "square" and within the measured boundaries. To be sure, it was a real fun and teaching time.

Then it happened! September 11, 2001, the United States of America was attacked by terrorists and thousands died in New York City and in Washington, DC. Personally it was a very scary time for me not knowing if my son and his wife were on those planes. Dave is a pilot and his wife, a flight attendant for the same airline. I rushed to their home and found them both safe and sound on their off-days, and we watched with grief as we saw the towers collapse. Two days later Dave, as a Navy pilot, was assigned to fly out of the Willow Grove Naval Base near Philadelphia and go to the Midwest to pick up rescue equipment. It was an eerie time for him as there were no other planes in the air. Within two weeks he was flying in the Middle East.

With such a tragedy, our nation was called to prayer. Personally, I was really in a quandary. Should I even think of flying on the 27th? Missionaries in Italy had asked me to come and teach Creation to their congregation and to several small groups as well. I had my ticket. Close friends prayed for me. Searching the scriptures I found in Psalm 18:29, "For by Thee I have run through a troop; and by my God have I leaped over a wall." Verse 32 continues, "It is God that girdeth me with strength and maketh my way perfect." So, I went!

The Italian people were so receptive and the missionaries kept me busy in their meetings and also in small classes. My flights were fine with no incidents. When I had to fly in my ministry, I always carried with me a small journal something like our old-fashioned "autograph books". I would send the book up to the pilot and have him fill in the stats of the flight and then sign his name. Sometimes a pilot would write a little message back to me. This provided a log of my flights. On my return home to Washington, D.C., the pilot wrote: "Welcome on board, Margaret. I was the pilot who flew you to Italy three weeks ago. Now I am bringing you back home!"

During Thanksgiving week I was at a retreat in the mountains of Georgia. International students were there from at least seventeen different countries. We witnessed two Korean young men accept the Lord at our table on Thanksgiving Day.

Rudi, a young Chinese man from Indonesia was with me as we talked to the men. Rudi, a one year Christian, prayed with them. What a blessing it was to be there and to do most of the teaching.

On my way home in northern South Carolina, I sensed that something was drastically wrong with my car. Out of the corner of my eye I had caught a glimpse of a service station sign. By this time all the red lights came on my dash board. I saw a ramp up ahead and aimed the car for the exit off the interstate. There was enough momentum for me to get to the top of the ramp and there my car died right at the stop sign. A car was coming up behind me. My electric windows didn't work and I tried to signal to the driver that he should go around me. He did. Then I saw this huge long tractor trailer headed right for me, full speed. I prayed that he wouldn't smash into me. The driver did slow up and decided to try to go around me. He drove out into the country road and making a wide turn, avoided even a scratch on my car. Grabbing my purse, I quickly left my vehicle and started to walk down the hill and along side a big ditch. I saw the service station at the bottom of the hill, kept walking and once in awhile looked back at my car sitting at the stop sign.

As I entered the main entrance to the service station a tall uniformed man stood there in front of me. He was a policeman on duty! I told him my plight. He offered to take me to a AAA service station. His police car was outside; I felt it was legitimate. So I got in his car and he drove me to another station a mile away. That manager retrieved my car and brought it down the hill without any brakes! I didn't want to look! He discovered that my universal belt had broken and he didn't have one. So he drove to a nearby town to get one for me, came back, fixed the car, charged the battery and I was on my way in two and half hours.

I was convinced that the Lord knew I needed help and He had the policeman right there waiting for me. He also provided a service man who even wanted to take me to get lunch at a local diner. In spite of my delay and detour, God was there! He provided!

Yes, every year of my life has been special but 2001 was a year to remember!

Cancer Support Group
Chapter 28

I mentioned the diagnosis of breast cancer in the last chapter "The Year—2001". At that same time I was caring for a man in his mid-sixties who was diagnosed with colon cancer. He was a member of our church and needed personal support. We both wondered if there were others in the church living with cancer. He lost his battle for life the following year.

The thought still pervaded my mind as I remembered the conversations we had about other people being afflicted. One Sunday evening I went to our senior pastor and told him that I had a burden to start a cancer support group. He replied, "Go for it!"

I knew a few folks who had some cancer histories and were survivors, so we had our first meeting. Five were present. This was on November 11, 2002.

One of the five was my friend Ellen Rauscher who continues to be in remission from a serious melanoma. She is my co-leader. We meet once a month in our church. We now have patients coming from at least seven churches.

Presently our prayer list has grown from five people to one hundred and fifty-two. There are now over fifty people on our active cancer list and the rest are in remission for now. No one is put on the list unless we have permission from the patient.

We also ask for their address and phone number so we can keep in touch with them about every three or four weeks. We keep a file on each one and pray that we will be an encouragement to them as we stay in touch with them. Ellen sends a special card and a cancer gospel tract to every new patient. Friendships are developed over the phone as we make contacts. Some are able to attend our meetings. Every month a new prayer list is made with updates.

Our meetings start with prayer. Then we sing. Music is a great therapy! One lady is in charge of the music, picks appropriate heart touching hymns and provides us with copies for every one. Then we have a devotional time with scripture. Our theme verse is Job 23:10:

"But He knows the way that I take: when He has tried me, I shall come forth as gold." We may read a chapter from a book written by a cancer patient and have started a library of research and life stories of those who went through treatment. Other times we have a special speaker. Recently we did a series of studies, a chapter at a time, of the DVD "Psalm 23 and Cancer" filmed and narrated in Israel by Dr. Ken Curtis.

Following our study and sharing time we regroup for prayer. After we review the new prayer list, we go in groups of three or four and actually pray for those under treatment. A social time follows and then we have a great time of fellowship as we share our past several weeks. Once a year we have a picnic! Folks help with refreshments, one lady makes reminder phone calls, and another is in charge of our library. Ellen, my co-leader, prints our monthly prayer list. It is really a team effort as we work together. I needed to mention this wonderful group of folks in this memoir because it has become a major part of my retirement years and has been a rewarding ministry as we work together serving our Lord Jesus.

Saga of the Thirty-Six Pine Trees

CHAPTER 29

It hit me hard, like a ton of bricks. One bright blue sunny day I walked for my morning exercise. I entered into a small cul-de-sac of private homes just down the street from me. I briefly glanced over to my right. "It's unbelievable!" I said to myself. For years I have never given thought to that border of trees on a lot which used to be ours. I stopped in my tracks and counted the best that I could, thirty-six pine trees which had been planted for a purpose. "We'll build a tennis court there some day," exclaimed my wonderful husband. Gone for almost twenty-one years and living where the Tree of Life grows, he is not in any way caring about those trees now.

I remember the day he planted them. He had a package of some three dozen little stems sporting a few roots. As I recall, he got them through some special "Plant a Tree for Beauty" program. With guideposts and rope he measured from one spot to the next. Planting had to be exactly perfect. Down on his knees he dug a hole and tenderly placed each little plant securely in place. Repeating this dozens of times, he measured and then dug the next hole.

If only he could see those trees today. Standing like giants reaching to heaven, making a green fence, they are guarding a "might have been" tennis court. The property no longer belongs to me and the trees remain a silent witness to a young husband, father, athlete who one day had a dream.

When I helped him plant trees on our regular rectangular lot every step was precise. The hole had to be just the right depth. Dig a little, lift the tree in, lift it out, dig some more, finally put the tree back in. Good dirt went over half of the roots. Then a big bucket of water, "Let the water seep in- that's good for the soil." The top half of the soil was added with some firm pats. When he stood up he would always pray, "May the Lord add His Blessing." He prayed over every tree.

And the Lord did add His blessing. One day recently I counted sixteen trees in the back yard, eleven in the side of the house, and nineteen down front. A total of forty-six trees. Some had been lost in storm or drought but these remaining trees faithfully grace the property. Springtime has always been a show time for some of them. Ablaze with deep pink, the flowering Crab Apples have cheered many a heart. One Weeping Cherry likes to send a pink radiance right through the window into the living room. Year round the great sturdy Oaks reach into the sky like mighty warriors. Silver Maples, some sixty to eighty feet tall always provide welcome shade. Three remaining fruit trees stand in their old age.

Special to me are three remaining pine trees in our front yard. I named them my trinity, representing the Father, the Son and the Holy Spirit. High and lofty they have grown into each other and remind me of 1 John 5:7 - "For there are three that bear record in heaven, the Father, the Word, and the Holy Ghost. And these three are one."

That day last summer when my eyes glanced over to those stately pines on the empty lot, my mind was challenged to remember that my husband's labor was not in vain. The trees he planted live on.

You can be sure that after I wrote the above in January of 2007, that I faced a very painful day in the spring of the same year. The builder who bought my lower two lots, came with his tree surgeons and cut down nine of the trees in the front yard. He planned to build two houses and it was inevitable that the trees had to go. I didn't want to watch so I left before they started with their saws. I knew we had to move on in life and this was a big hurdle.

However there is a tree I am very anxious to see. It is mentioned in the book of Revelation 22:2 - "… and on the either side of the river, was there a tree of life, which bare twelve manner of fruits, and yielded her fruit every month: and the leaves of the tree were for the healing of the nations."

Now I am wondering, will there be any pine trees in heaven?

The Big Move
Chapter 30

A widow is left to do everything! Sometimes I despaired when the maintenance chores overwhelmed me. The youth at our church, under the leadership of our youth pastors, came a few times to do some major jobs. One project was absolute fun for them. Have you ever heard of demolition crews? Car loads of young men came with their axes and hammers, rakes and shovels. In just a few hours they literally removed a garden shed which had deteriorated. What fun! Smash! Bang! Rake! Haul!

Another time they came and raked the entire property. After filling gigantic tarps with fallen leaves, they marched nine abreast, hauling their loads over to the side of the road for pick-up!

Two families in our church provided five young boys who came on a regular basis to trim shrubs and to mow around trees and flower beds. When one boy went off to college, the next in-line brother took over. I usually did the tractor mowing!

I felt for a long time that it was worth keeping the property. We had so many wonderful memories! When my husband was still living we had a neighbor picnic every summer. Our children went door to door to invite families to come. One year we had ninety-two people! Another year it poured down rain and we all scooted into the house and down into the cellar. (That is what western Pennsylvania people call a basement)

Don built a back stop on our property across the street and with base plates officially laid, there was always a softball game to remember! At our neighbor picnics it was possible to have fifteen or twenty people on each team. After the ball game we had some sort of a program, singing, slide shows, or a neighbor family would perform. It was always a great time to get to know your neighbors.

The inside meetings are also very special in my memory. Family dinners, dinners with friends, committee meetings, the early days of Young at Heart Meetings (until we had no more room), Christmas gatherings, widow's luncheons, meals with speakers at church. Missionary families often stayed with us which broadened our horizons.

One of our wedding gifts back in 1950 was a guest book. We decided to use it from the start and so anytime people came to visit, we had them sign our book. It is such a blessing to look back over the many books with records of past friends and relatives who came into our home. Presently we are using our eighth book and it was started after I moved here to my present abode.

One day in November of 2006 was a very sad day. It was bitter cold. Bundled up with slacks, sweater, jacket, hat, scarf and gloves, I drove our tractor (20 HP, 60 inch cut) around our property. *Maybe this will be my last time to mow this year?* I was driving down the right hand side of my property, watching that I didn't hit any tree roots. The wind howled. I looked up right into the sky and said, "Lord, how long will I have to do this?" Tears flowed freely down my face. As I got closer to the bank and the main street, I thought to myself, *"Margaret, you better straighten up. There's lots of traffic on South Main Street. If someone drives by and sees you bawling they'll call 911! They will think that old lady is sick or in pain!"*

So, I got my composure, finished my job, parked the mower in the garage and entered my cozy home. I knew that in God's time I would sell the house and move!

Three years prior to moving I attended a seminar at our local hospital. The class was designed for senior citizens. The subject—Downsizing! I had been doing that. We were told that if we had a schedule and just worked a few hours a week that we would be surprised at what we could accomplish. I gave away dishes, serving plates, quilts, blankets, books, (over 300) encylopedias (a missionary took these for Costa Rica), pieces of furniture I was not using, clothes I never wore. This preparation helped me so much when I did move from 719 S. Main Street.

So the move was already in progress. The actual move started on Tuesday July 3, 2007, after I heard that my apartment was ready at the Rockhill Mennonite Community in Sellersville, Pennsylvania. Crew number one arrived with two trucks. Bob Behn, then chairman of our trustee board at church, organized the men. On July 5, another crew moved "stuff". It rained all that day and the plan was to move my bed which, of course, meant my mattress could be soaked along with the other furniture. They were evening crews and by six o'clock I thought it would be best to cancel the plan. My son Dan said, "Mother, wait and see what will happen. Let's see what God will do." As the men came at seven o'clock, the rain stopped and there was only a very slight drizzle. We talked about what to do and the group decided to pack up the truck. At nine o'clock, when we finished for the evening, the rain came again and it rained all night. We knew that God was with us! Altogether there were fifteen different groups of men and women who came at their various times to help pack, lift, transport, move me in, hang pictures, clean and did it with loving spirits. There were thirty-five of them plus my six family members and that made forty-one willing hands. What a blessing this was. Many an evening I was so weary but I claimed the verse, "They that wait upon the Lord, shall renew their strength; they shall mount up with wings as eagles; they shall run and not be weary; they shall walk and not faint." (Isaiah 40:31)

By August I was settled in and enjoying this wonderful place. I sat at my prayer table on the sun porch. I stopped reading my devotional to meditate. I looked out the side window and to my right saw something there by the large retention pond that had been built for state regulations. Casually I returned to what I was reading and I began to think *Did I really see a gazebo sitting there?* It was a real gazebo and I wrote about it in this little article which was published in one of our news letters.

"Surprise!"

My godly parents loved gardening, flowers, and the out-of-doors. My father would be out in the vegetable garden tilling the ground, planting the seedlings, tying up the tomato plants from morning until evening. He and his brother built a greenhouse on our property. They eeked out an existence during the depression as they sold small vegetable and flower plants. So it seemed appropriate when my parents were both gone and my brother Robert sold our family home that with some of my inheritance I bought a gazebo in their memory. It graced our property for at least fifteen years and reminded me of my marvelous heritage. Then came the time for me, as a widow, to sell my house and move into a retirement community. The gazebo was included in the sale of the house.

My new apartment is high on the fourth floor. Four days ago I was in the summer and winter sun porch reading the Bible. I glanced to my side and looked down and thought,"Am I seeing what I think I see?" I blinked and looked again. Sure

The DeLancey Gazebo

enough there was a gazebo on the side of the pond being constructed. When I inquired I was told that it had been there less than twenty-four hours. There will be a walking path right to the entrance and the gazebo will be for all the residents to enjoy.

Yes, I know the gazebo is there for all of us to appreciate, but last Friday my heart cried out,"God has given ME a gazebo. My heritage lives on!"

(Written by Margaret DeLancey August 21, 2007)

Obviously God was behind these scenes and was directing my paths. I am now settled in and enjoying my new home with so many amenities. On Monday mornings in the spring, summer and fall, I waken to hear the drone of the commercial mowers and I am not doing the grass cutting! Praise the Lord!

Changes
Chapter 31

One morning this past October, I looked out my fourth floor bedroom window. The view is always beautiful especially the gorgeous sunsets. However the scene caught me by surprise! The leaves had changed color! *When did that happen? Overnight?* I had not observed the slow change of the green leaves to brilliant shades of yellow, red and orange. I am sure they changed gradually. I was just not observant.

The experience brought to my mind about changes in my personal life. Memories darted from the past and I started to list them. I remembered:

- Clamp on roller skates (had to use a key)
- Saddle shoes and socks
- Clothes lines
- Double washing machines, ringers, double rinse tubs
- Weekly Saturday night baths
- Itchy "footie" pajamas
- Walking to school
- Writing tablets with a map of Pennsylvania on the front

- Lead pencils # 2
- Large veggie gardens
- Making root beer and sauerkraut in the cellar
- Hand "warshing" all pans and "deeshes"
- Fall apple butter festivals in Grandmother Elliott's back yard
- Party phone lines
- Black and white television- three channels
- Hand me downs for our new wardrobe
- Popcorn balls and an orange for a Christmas treat
- Long stockings with a garter belt
- Pigtails with bows or "rag" curls

- Playing jacks at the kitchen table
- Jumping rope at recess
- "Redding" up our rooms (cleaning, making ready)
- Eating buns, putting things in pokes, drinking pop, using gum bands (all Western Pennsylvania language)
- Liverwurst sandwiches
- Ring bologna, boiled and pecan rolls on Sunday mornings
- Cleaning carpets on the clothes lines; carpet beaters (playing tag and hiding inside the carpets)
- Quarantine signs on front porch doors- Measles, Mumps, Scarlet Fever, Chicken Pox, Diphtheria.

- Cloth diapers
- Doctor's house calls
- Smells of bread "rising" and then baking in the oven

- Making fudge on a rainy day
- Cooking the blue laundry starch on Mondays- always the wash day
- Cleaning the fish pond once a year
- Dashing through the sprinklers on a hot day
- Helping Mother put the lace curtains on the stretcher to dry

- Wearing wool bathing suits that softened up when wet
- Car sick episodes (all six of us!)
- New dresses- "Made by Mother"
- First bought coat when in high school
- Black out drills when the fire whistle sounded
- Parading through the vacation camp ground in Ohio when World War 11 was declared to be over. Pots and pans and all noise makers used to celebrate

All on the list shaped and molded my life as I grew up from that little baby girl born in 1928. Through these changes godly and praying parents were a treasure. My parents raised all of us by prayer, perseverance, living through the Great Depression and being wonderful Christian living examples to follow. Now they have been in heaven two and three decades and to whom do we now look? There have been many changes in all of our lives; some have been good, some bad, some sad, some beneficial for our growth, some making us stronger in our walk.

Changes occur in:

Our plans and desires

Our looks (one glance in the mirror will tell you)

Our ways of living
(maybe slowing down a bit and not running)
Our residences (many of us have moved)
Our health
Our finances

Despite the changes there is One who never changes. The hymn writer wrote, "Oh, thou who changes not, abide with me." What an anchor we have!

Malachi 3:6 - "For I am the Lord, I change not"

Hebrews 13:8 - "Jesus Christ, the same yesterday, today and for ever."

Departures
Chapter 32

I never liked "goodbyes". Vivid memories return as I think about my children who came for holidays and reunions. After days of fun and laughter, they packed up and off they went. I understood they had to get back to their homes and jobs, but it was always sad.

My sisters tried to come once a year for several days and when they left we would always shed some tears. You must understand that we were naturally big "cry babies"!

I would watch as precious ones backed out of the driveway, drive a short distance to the stop sign, make a left turn and drive out of sight. Then I remembered what my mother had told me many years ago.

She explained to me how sad she would always be when Don and I and the children left after a visit to Grandma and Grandpap's. Their house was then so quiet and lonely. She would enlist my two sisters to start the cleanup. Change beds, dust, and vacuum. As I remember those departure days I realized that there have been some very sad final departures in my life.

The first departure was my father-in-law, Lawrence DeLancey. He was the head of the shipping department of the US Gauge Company in Sellersville. Even though he had a lot of responsibility, he was a jolly man. He relaxed from the pressures of his job by raising and selling prize bantam roosters. He departed this life after suffering a massive stroke. Determined to get home, he stumbled across the street from his plant, staggered up the front steps, entered his house, sat in his favorite chair and never woke up. Twelve hours later in the hospital, he met his Savior.

Lawrence Abraham DeLancey, September 12, 1894-April 23, 1958

The second sad departure came when I was enjoying a nice weekend in Ohio with Rebekah and her husband Gary. Mid morning a call came from my mother. "William is gone!" I was shocked. He was the next child after me—we grew up together. I had just talked to him a few days before. He was discharged from the hospital and had a heart attack at home. My plane ticket was changed and I flew to Pittsburgh instead of back to Philadelphia. The waiting room in the airport was full of travelers. I sat alone and as I thought of my brother, the tears flowed. I blew my nose, got control, and then the flood started all over again. No one in that one hour of waiting asked if they could help! "No one cared for my soul"! God taught me a real lesson that day. Never, ever, let someone sorrow without offering your kind words of help and comfort!

After his funeral, we gathered for a large family meal. I was asked to pray and the only thing I could pray was, "Surely he hath borne our griefs and carried our sorrows" (Isaiah 53:4). The Lord healed and we remember William fondly.

William Edward Wunderley, January 12, 1931-April 28, 1979

The third one who left was Mother DeLancey, Don's mother. Martha was a lady very well known in the community of Sellersville, Pennsylvania. She was especially popular at Christmas time. Her parents built a special Christmas putz that took up two front rooms in the large brick home next door. One year there were 10,000 people who came to see it. They hailed from twenty-two different states. After they saw the putz which involved moving trains, mechanized people going in and out of the church, manger and shepherd scenes, they would go next door to see Martha's Christmas tree.

All year long she collected combs, pencils, writing pads, pictures, bracelets, crayons, small story books, beautiful handkerchiefs and many other items. Each was wrapped, with the appropriate age marked on the outside. Along with the gift was a gospel tract telling the real story of Christmas. These gifts were hung on a white tree which was basically a large limb with branches, painted white and secured in a stand –up base. (I recently learned that our local state representative, Mr. Paul Clymer, had purchased this unique display tree when we sold her home and had a public sale. He uses it once in awhile for special events.) Even the local kindergarten children came with their teachers to receive a gift from the special tree.

Martha lived in her cute bungalow home after Dad passed on. She worked for a time and stayed independent. But then Martha broke her hip and was unable to live alone.

She lived with us for three years. One Saturday morning she went unconscious and on Monday morning, in the hospital, she went into His presence.

Martha Heinrichs-DeLancey, January 24, 1895-June 25, 1979

The fourth departure was my absolutely wonderful father whom we lovingly called "Daddy". Oldest of a family of seven boys and one girl (an 8th boy died in infancy), he learned to cook, clean, bake bread, and scrub floors. An industrious man, he continued to learn even though he had to drop out of school to go to work. He and his brothers were carpenters and Daddy worked hard as a foreman in a lumber company. A public servant and a born leader, he was a Sunday School teacher, and an elder in the Liberty Presbyterian Church in our little borough. Known as a public speaker, he was also a record holder for the number of years he served on the local school board. During the depression he and his brother Lou built a greenhouse on our property. They were able to sell vegetable and flower plants, and this helped with some income to keep food on the table. He loved to garden.

His favorite hymn was "In the Garden". One fall day as he was roto-tilling his plot he was making crooked lines. His brother Lou came from next door and told him to correct his rows. Uncle Lou turned to go back to his house and Daddy fell to the ground and his roto-tiller kept going out of the garden and up to a row of bushes. Daddy departed suddenly and into the arms of Jesus. So- he met the Lord in the garden!

William George Wunderley, October 12, 1904-November 1, 1984

My dear husband was the fifth who departed. We have already told you about my precious husband in the chapter entitled "Duke the Dentist". His departure was peaceful as his body functions stopped and he was ushered into glory. I often wonder if people use their musical talents in heaven. People flippantly talk about playing harps up yonder. I am sure that Don is there worshipping the Lamb whether he is playing an instrument or using his beautiful tenor voice. We still miss him dearly, and know we, who remain, may also go sooner than we think.

Donald Ellis DeLancey, February 29, 1924-March 2, 1986

The sixth one to leave was my brother Reuel. I knew he was so sick. He was fighting a lung cancer called Mesothelioma. Three months after we buried my husband, I drove to Pittsburgh to see him. We shared some precious times together. Reuel Pardee was named after two wonderful Christian endeavor friends of my parents—William Pardee and Reuel Wolford. Reuel was the life of the party. He was the one with the jokes that kept us laughing. He departed this life when I was in Israel with my broken leg; I could not come home for the funeral. Reuel was esteemed highly in the community of Liberty Borough. The government officials there named a ball park facility after him. Now we had two wonderful brothers in heaven.

Reuel Pardee Wunderley, July 12, 1933-July 26, 1986

My precious mother was the seventh one to go. She was the most wonderful, loving, and understanding person. I was always the proudest child in our school when she came to visit. In my growing up years, a week of school was opened to random visits from the parents. The classroom door opened and in walked this beautiful lady all dressed up with a hat, gloves, and purse. She was MY mother! She saw me through all my high school years, and when I married and moved three hundred miles away, she wrote me encouraging letters. She came and helped me with my last three babies. She was with me when Don died!

Mother came for visits and stayed for weeks at a time. You may remember reading about our time in California when you read "Riding the Rails". We had a wonderful mother-daughter relationship. Her departure came after a two-month battle with liver cancer. Faith and Howard lovingly cared for mother in their home during those last days. Roselaine and Harold, Robert and Judy also assisted as well as other members of the family. After she died, it was a sad and challenging time-days and weeks, when we cleaned out the only home we ever knew. It helped us to know she was in heaven with Jesus and with Daddy.

Alma Rosella Elliot-Wunderley, August 22, 1904-January 24, 1990

There have been other departures in our extended family, like our sweet sisters-in law, Clarabelle and Judy, but we will conclude with the ones listed above because it would be many if we included grandparents, aunts and uncles. But I do want to mention three special departures of grandfathers:

Great-Grandfather Johann Christian Wunderlich (Wunderley) died December 22, 1875. He was skating on the river and carried a prized possession. He had purchased a pig and was taking it home to be cooked for the big Christmas dinner. The ice broke open underneath him and he slipped into the cold waters of the Youghiogheny and died.

My grandfather Edward S. Elliott suffered from a paralyzing stroke. He was an invalid for many months. In those days, people were kept in their homes and cared for by their family. My mother said that when he passed away, she and her sister Aunt Gertrude were attending, one on his right side and the other on his left. They held Grandpap's hands. When he departed he smiled and raised his paralyzed arms toward the ceiling taking their hands with him. He must have seen the Lord or had a glimpse of heaven. Then he dropped his arms and he was gone.

Grandfather Heinrichs, Don's grandfather was breathing his last breaths. The family thought he was gone. Then he opened his eyes and said that he wanted to tell the whole family what he saw. They gathered around and he said that it was indescribable. He told of the glories of heaven and said that he hoped everyone would be able to go there. Then he closed his eyes and breathed his last.

This may have been for some a very morbid chapter, but it should bring us great hope in the Lord. We shall see the King one day and our faith will become sight. "He that believeth in Him shall not perish but shall have everlasting life." (John 3:16)

Hallelujah!

Finally Home
Chapter 33

As I look back on my life I remember one evening at church when my husband was still living. An evangelist from Word of Life was there for the week and this particular evening was the night we had our youth clubs. We were all challenged after the meeting to be fully surrendered to the Lord and His leading in our lives. The closing hymn for that evening was "Have Thine own way, Lord, Have Thine own way. You are the potter, I am the clay." I was convicted to go up front and stand with some of the girls who wanted to dedicate their lives to the Lord. I also wanted to testify that I wanted to be obedient to the Lord in my future service for Him. It was like a renewal for me as I yielded to the leading of the Holy Spirit. When the service was over, my husband asked me why I had done this. I explained that I wanted to be fully surrendered to the Lord. Little did I know that mid-life the Lord's plan for me was to be a widow.

Therefore I praise the Lord for the ministries He gave me and all the opportunities and travels that I have had in my lifetime and since I have been single again. North, south, east, and west, in all directions I have traveled but the best trip is yet to come. "But as it is written, Eye hath not seen, nor ear heard, neither have entered into the heart of man the things that God hath prepared for them that love him." (I Corinthians 2:9) When our dear sister in Christ, Ruth Myers, died in June of 2009, I sat that morning and imagined what it might have been like for her and wrote the following:

"It's Beautiful"

I left on Saturday morning! I suppose I never woke up. Just so quickly the angels carried me here. It's all so exciting! And I thought that going down the Delaware on a tube and falling into a pond in Indonesia was so super fun. I can hardly wait until you come and join me. I do know that you have work to do on earth and you will come when God calls.

The air is so wonderful. I can breathe! No more tubes in my nose and chest. I can walk, too. I don't see wheelchairs or walkers. My mind is clear. I feel like singing praises.

But the most amazing thing is that I saw Jesus for the first time! He even said, "Welcome home, Ruth!" Then I saw this beautiful indescribable place and looked around. Angels and people everywhere. I heard them call each other "Saint"! I am not sure just when I will find Russell. He is here somewhere. This is just wonderful.

Be glad for me. And, I will be watching for you!

Love and prayers, Mother Ruth

The above was just my finite mind at work. We have no promise of whether we leave a sick bed or suddenly step over into glory with a sudden attack or a car accident. God has a plan for our lives and He is in control. Aunt Ruth wished she could go in her sleep and she did! We have the promise to be absent from the body and to be present with the Lord! (2 Corinthians 5:8) The best scenario would be if the Lord came in our life time and just took us to glory. "Then we which are alive and remain shall be caught up together with them in the clouds to meet the Lord in the air: and so shall we ever be with the Lord. (I Thessalonians 4:17)

One of my husband's favorite speakers in the nineteen-fifties was Dr. Harry Rimmer. He was a great Bible teacher and was able to make the Bible live when he preached. He was also a scientist and an archaeologist and his lectures on science and the Bible have long been remembered.

Dr. Rimmer spent his last days in California after a diagnosis of a terminal cancer. Each Saturday he listened to the radio and heard his good friend preach. This friend was Dr. Charles Fuller who announced that on the next Sunday he would be preaching on his favorite subject- Heaven.

Dr. Rimmer wrote to Dr. Fuller:

My dear Charlie:

Next Sunday you are to talk about heaven. I am interested in that land because I have a clear title to a bit of property there for over 50 years. I did not buy it, for it was given to me without money and with out price. But the donor purchased it for me at a tremendous cost. I am not holding it for speculation, for the deed is not transferable.. It is not a vacant lot, for I have been sending material there for over fifty years of which the greatest Architect and Builder of the Universe has been building a home for me which will suit me perfectly and will never need to be repaired. Termites cannot undermine its foundations, for it rests on the "Rock of Ages". Fire cannot destroy it. Floods cannot wash it away. No locks or bolts will ever be placed on the doors for no devious person can ever enter that land where my dwelling stands, almost completed. It is ready for me to enter in rest in peace internally without fear of being ejected. There is a Valley of deep shadow between the place where I live in California and that to which I shall journey in a short time. I cannot reach my home in that city of gold without passing through the dark shadows. But, I am not afraid because the best Friend I ever had went through the same valley long ago, and drove away its gloom. He has stuck with me through thick and thin since we first became acquainted fifty- five years ago, and I hold His promise in printed form never to forsake me nor to leave me alone. He will be with me as I walk through the valley of the shadows, and I shall not lose my way when He is with me.

I hope to hear your sermon on Sunday next from my home here, but I have no assurance that I shall. My ticket to Heaven has no date stamped upon it, no return coupon, and no permit for baggage. I am all ready to go, and I may not be here when you are talking next Sunday, but if not, I shall meet you there some day.

Signed,
Harry Rimmer, Sc.D

This letter was placed upon the desk of Dr. Fuller the next Wednesday. By that time Dr. Rimmer was already in that land which is fairer than day. The land that he had seen by faith for over 50 years.

(Dr. Rimmer's story was taken from Al Smith's *Treasury of Hymn Histories*, Heritage Music Distributors. Published 1981)

A dear nurse friend of mine related to me how she held the face of her dying husband and said to him, "Just think- you will soon see Jesus. He whispered softly his last words to her, "I can't wait!" How blessed it is when we have a hope beyond the grave.

So we all wait for that final call; there is no age limit. I think of the motto that we used to have in our home. "Only one life will soon be past. Only what's done for Christ will last." Am I so conceited that I believe I am super great and that is why I think I will go to heaven? No way!

As I look back on December 4, 1949, when I asked Jesus to forgive me and come into my life as Savior I know that is when I became a Christian. There has been lots of molding and making (ouch!) and I will not be complete until I hear the last call and be finally home! "He that believeth in him should not perish but have everlasting life." (John 3:16) What a promise we have. So until then I hope to see you here or there or in the air!

Glory!

John 14:1 "Let not your heart be troubled.
Ye believe in God, believe also in me."

John 14:2 "In my father's house are many mansions:
If it were not so, I would have told you."

John 14:6 "Jesus saith unto him, I am the way, the truth,
and the life: no man cometh to the Father but by me."

Gloria in Excelsis—Deo!

FINALLY HOME